Restoring
the withered
Soul

Inspire Publishing

First published in Australia in 2005

Copyright © Shane Willard 2005

Apart from any fair dealing for the purposes of private study, research, criticism or review, as permitted under the Copyright Act, no part may be reproduced by any process without written permission of both the copyright owner and the above publisher of this book.

www.inspirepublishing.org

ISBN: 0-9752315-5-3

Cover design by Ben Windle
Internal design and typeset by Andrew Steele

Printed and bound in Australia by Griffin Press, Australia.
Written in U.S. English.

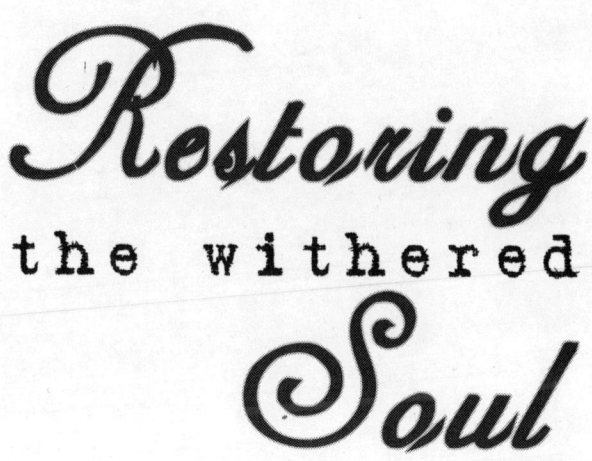

SHANE WILLARD

inspire
publishing

Contents

Chapter One
What is the Promise *of* Life?   1

Chapter Two
What is Our Make Up?   11

Chapter Three
Why is My Soul Sagging?   25

Chapter Four
How Can I Live From Friday to Sunday?   41

Chapter Five
The Resurrection Guarantee   57

Chapter Six
Do I Really Matter?   73

Chapter Seven
Shame "Off" You   87

Chapter Eight
Embracing Your Acceptance with God   99

Chapter Nine
Rebuilding Who You Really Are   111

Epilogue   125

WHAT IS THE PROMISE of LIFE?

I COULD HEAR PEOPLE SCREAMING. Patients would accost me saying, "Please help"; "Get me out of here." When I walked into the psychiatric ward of the hospital, a shocking feeling came over me. I could literally feel the oppression in the hall. The place felt so sad, depressed, angry, chaotic and hopeless. This experience changed my life because it framed a basic thought through which people filter God and their life with Him.

A woman who had six children from five different men was heavily addicted to both illegal and prescription drugs and had been through a tough time for years. There was so much pain on her face, and she cried and told me all sorts of violations that had come her way in her life. She had chosen to hide behind the feeling that drugs gave her. My heart was moved with compassion for her because she was understandably crying with some serious emotion. I put my arm around her and told her that Jesus loves her so much that He was collecting her tears in a bottle. She told me how much she loved Him too, but just could not seem to beat her addictions. Her next statement was part of the inspiration for this book. She said, "Shane, I understand heaven, hell and forgiveness. I understand someday my life with God will have nothing wrong with it, but I don't understand salvation for my life today."

I think her sentiments ring loudly with many of us. The church has unintentionally painted a picture of salvation as something with only eternal significance. We have painted this picture that screams the message, "Get saved!! One day you will die and it will all get better." This is evidenced in the songs we sing. Here is an example from one, "It will be worth it all, when we see Jesus. Life's trials will seem so small, when we see Christ." Is there anything untrue about the lyrics to that song? NO. However, it carries an undertone that is so prevalent amongst Christians. We are just trying to suffer for Jesus through our time on earth so that we can get to the promise in heaven.

This sentiment captures the greatness of salvation in eternity. Yes, we will spend eternity with our Creator. Yes, we will enjoy perfect fellowship with Him. Yes, we will rule on a new earth with the original intent of the Kingdom of God in operation. However, this sentiment misses the greatness of salvation — here, now, today. There are Christians that I have met everywhere who are working through the same thought. It sounds something like this, "I am so thankful for the promise of eternal life, but what about the promise of life, today?"

In John 10:10 Jesus makes an interesting statement regarding this dichotomy of eternal life versus life today. He said, "The thief comes only to steal and kill and destroy; I have come that they may have life, and have it to the full." It is almost like there is a collective scream from the followers of Christ that says, "What about that? What about the promise of abundant life? Surely God does not define abundant life as simply converting oxygen to carbon dioxide. Surely, there is more to life than what I am experiencing. There has to be!!!"

Taking this tension to the extreme can lead to a dangerous end. We scrutinize our life to the point where we become extremely sin-conscious. We tell ourselves that we should be experiencing abundant life and, if we are not, we must have something in our life that makes God mad. Remember when the disciples confronted Jesus with this very thing. They came across a man who was born blind, and assumed that some sin that manifested in blindness had influenced this man. Jesus said that no sin was responsible for his illness, but that glory should come to God through the illness being healed[1]. Once we fall into the trap of living sin-consciously, it is a huge slippery slope. The Bible declares that trying to maintain a relationship with God by keeping the law only creates sin-consciousness[2]. In other words, trying to live the abundant life by getting it all right will only make you aware of where you miss it. We will discuss more of this dynamic later in the book.

This tension between two separate ideas of quality of life is nothing new. For example, the Bible says that David was a man after God's own heart. If anyone should be experiencing abundant life, it should be a person that is 'after God's own heart'. At the same time, this man wrote something that demonstrates great pain in Psalm 22. He made a dual statement of his emotional state as well as a prophetic utterance of Messiah's suffering. He said, "My strength and my soul are withered up like a dried potsherd[3]." How does a man after God's own heart get to that emotional state? Have you ever been there? Have you ever been in the state the woman found herself in at the beginning of this chapter? Have you ever said what she found herself saying?

If so, then you have experienced something that everyone has experienced at some point. You have experienced a withered soul. The word David used in Psalm 22 is the Hebrew word *yabesh* which means *to make dry, to wither, to become withered, to exhibit dryness*. It is an unmistakable picture of something dying and would be the opposite of the image of life and life abundantly that Jesus is trying to communicate. For example, take a plant or a tree that is experiencing abundant life.

Chapter One

David said it this way in Psalm 1:

> *"Blessed is the man who does not walk in the counsel of the wicked or stand in the way of sinners or sit in the seat of mockers. But his delight is in the law of the* L<small>ORD</small>*, and on his law he meditates day and night. He is like a tree planted by streams of water, which yields its fruit in season and whose leaf **does not wither**. Whatever he does prospers."*

On one hand, you have a huge tree, full of fruit, green, pliable, with a large root base and a plentiful water supply. On the other hand, you have a withered tree that is like the chaff which the wind can drive away[4]. It is small, sagging, brown, brittle, has a weak root base, is fruitless and has a limited water supply.

David is using this word picture to communicate the dichotomy of how we live. Since we know that Jesus came that we could live in an abundant life, why do we feel small, insignificant, depressed, lifeless and isolated? What makes the smallest change break us in half? That is a withered soul. Why are we withering? What is the promise of life he talked about? Where is the life that is significant, full of life, joyful, connected and so flexible nothing could break it? When do we achieve it? How do we get it?

The good news is that David, who said his soul was withered, wrote an entirely different story in Psalm 23. He makes a statement that should breathe hope into every person that hears it, **"He restores my soul!"** The word David used there is *shoob*. This word has several meanings. One meaning is *to return*. God is in the business of returning our soul back to Him. He is changing our awareness from self-consciousness to God-consciousness. He is in the process of turning us from self-centered to God-centered.

Secondly, the word can mean *to refresh*. The heart of God refreshes our soul. God takes a set of thoughts, emotions and decisions that have become lifeless and refreshes it. He breathes new life into our thoughts. He breathes new life into our emotions. He breathes new life into our direction. He refreshes us. Sometimes, when we find ourselves in a withered emotional state, we need refreshing more than correction.

Years ago, I was going through something that made me feel as if I was dying. I was in my early twenties, and circumstances led me to a place where everything important to me at the time disappeared. Looking back on the situation now, it was really no big deal because it was temporary, but in the moment it felt like a big deal. When something feels like a big deal, then it is a big deal to the person who feels it. My soul literally felt like it was withering slowly. God provided an unexpected encounter with my mentor over a four-day period of time that really revitalized me. He did not correct me because I already knew where I was wrong. However, he was used by God to totally refresh me. We met for four hours per night for four straight days. I left his hotel room after four days with refreshed thoughts, emotions, visions and beliefs. Out of seven billion people in the world, God decided to show up in a hotel room in North Charleston, South Carolina just for me. This is the heart of God to restore the soul.

The third meaning of *shoob* is *to repair*. This is the same idea as setting a broken bone. During a 'touch' football game in eighth grade, I saw someone break his arm badly. He went airborne to catch a pass and got hit on his feet. The hit flipped him head long, and he instinctively put his arm down to brace the fall. The arm did not make it. We heard it snap. His arm literally had a huge bend. After x-rays to confirm the break, the doctor pulled his arm straight to set the bone. The patient screamed in pain, but the doctor had just made it possible for his arm to be restored. Without the pain of setting the bone, the patient's arm would have been useless for life.

The picture of setting a broken bone is appropriate for what God is saying in Psalm 23. He is saying that He is willing to see us through a process of pain in order to restore usefulness to our soul. Either our thoughts and emotions are working to bring us into a greater awareness of God and what He has for us, or they are working to make us more self-conscious. God's heart is to repair the places that make us self-conscious by replacing it with awareness of Him. He will restore our soul.

I invite you over the course of reading this book to journey with me in discovering just how God takes a man whose soul is withered and turns him into a man who proclaims loudly, "My soul is restored." What does that process look like? How can I make sure I am in on it? Friend, the heart of our Creator is for our soul to experience His peace and life.

Endnotes
1. John 9:1-12
2. Romans 3:20
3. Psalm 22:15
4. Psalm 1:4

WHAT IS OUR MAKE UP?

What is Our Make Up?

When I was in Bible College, we had to attend chapel every day. I was sitting in a typical Bible college chapel service when an announcement was made from the stage that one of the key faculty members would be missing the rest of the year due to depression. I sat in my perch in the balcony that day and cast some serious judgments against that faculty member. In a moment, a conglomeration of ignorance went through my mind at the speed of light. Thoughts ran through my mind like, "How can he really trust God and be depressed?"; "What about the joy of the Lord?"; "Doesn't he know that God is in control?"; "Doesn't he know that God works all things together for good?"

Do any of these questions sound familiar? We do this sort of thing all the time. We cast judgments based on incredible ignorance. Listen to the pride in some of the questions running through my mind. "How can he really trust God and be depressed?" In other words, I really trust God, and I am not depressed. Therefore, if he is depressed, then he must not trust God. This assumes that my immediate state of mind becomes the rule for all human beings. How ignorant, insensitive and unloving can a person be? However, we make conclusions about people based on circumstances and behavior rather than substance, faith and fruit.

At least three things are cyclical in nature. In other words, they return to us — blessings, curses and judgments. We are made in the image and likeness of God which means that the same principles that govern the heavenlies, govern us. The Bible says that God's Word does not return void. The principle is that God's Word returns. When God speaks, His words carry authority and return to Him with power. God actually feels the effects of the power of His words. This power is never void.

Likewise, our words return to us with power. Jesus said it this way:

> *"Do not judge, or you too will be judged. For in the same way you judge others, you will be judged, and with the measure you use, it will be measured to you. "Why do you look at the speck of sawdust in your brother's eye and pay no attention to the plank in your own eye? How can you say to your brother, 'Let me take the speck out of your eye,' when all the time there is a plank in your own eye? You hypocrite, first take the plank out of your own eye, and then you will see clearly to remove the speck from your brother's eye…So in everything, do to others what you would have them do to you, for this sums up the Law and the Prophets[1]."*

When we cast judgment, those words return to us with the same power and standard we used to cast the judgment. That is powerful to think about. This held true in my life with the judgment I cast against the faculty member with depression. Three months later, I began to lose weight rapidly, and I felt inexplicably sad for really no reason. I became so depressed that I had to go to the doctor. I just could not beat it. In the middle of my depression, I remembered what I had said to myself about the faculty member. Those same thoughts began to go through my mind about myself. "Where is my faith? Can I really trust God and feel depressed?" The same measure I used to judge the faculty member with depression returned on my head. This can go so far. We have all heard people say things in judgment about other people's circumstances that they have to live with themselves later. It is a principle of the spirit; our words return to us. I thank God for lifting the depression in a relatively short period. However, the judgment cycle still affected me.

I failed to understand the basic make-up of all human beings. We are made in the image and likeness of God. God is three dimensional, so we are three dimensional. We are spirit, soul and body. This helps explain why it is possible for people to love God with all their heart, but they are as crazy as an orangutan.

You are a Spirit

The Bible says that our truest essence is our spirit being[2]. God is a Spirit, and we are in His likeness. The word for likeness is *demooth* which carries the connotation of kind. We are in the similitude, manner and likeness of God. Since His essence is spirit, then our essence is spirit. Our spirit defines who we really are. It is perfectly natural for us to be spiritual. We cannot be more spiritual than spirit any more than someone can be more woman than woman or more man than man. Unfortunately, this is not always what we reflect to the world, but, nonetheless, it is who we really are. Our substance is defined by it.

Much of the problem of the withered soul is that we define ourselves out of our flesh rather than by our substance. We can tend to define ourselves by behavior, looks, intelligence and an assortment of facets that are not the true substance of our being. The way we define ourselves affects everything. I was on a trip once with a guy who just assumed the whole group did not mind putting the coffee pot on while he was in the shower, so another guy with us decided to teach him a lesson. He put his coffee in the filter, but, before he ran the water through it, he put a used gym sock in the filter. The coffee was still coffee, but the flavor tasted like a gym sock. Our substance is defined by the coffee, but our flavor is defined by the filter.

Our life with God is much like that. Our substance is defined by our spirit which is our truest essence. The Bible defines our spirit by some incredible statements —"Christ in you is the hope of glory[3]"; "For me to live **is** Christ, and to die is gain[4]"; "My life is hidden in Christ[5]"; "When Christ, who **is** my life shall appear, I shall also appear with Him in glory[6]"; "Christ is fused to my spirit[7]". All of these statements are absolutely incredible.

"Christ in you, the hope of glory." Think about that statement. Christ is in me. All He is, all He was, and all He will ever be exists in my spirit right now. This fact is my only 'hope of glory'. The word *glory* can be traced back to the word translated *image* in Genesis. In other words, the only hope of reflecting the image God originally intended for me is that all of Christ defines my spirit.

"For me to live **is** Christ"; "When Christ who **is** my life shall appear." The verb comes from the root *to be*. In other words, Paul is saying that my being is defined by Christ. My being is defined by the same things that define Christ — love, joy, peace, longsuffering, gentleness, goodness, meekness, self-control, grace, compassion, slow to anger, abounding in love, forgiving all kinds of wickedness, rebellion and sin[8,9]. My substance finds all of its assets and abilities in the person of Christ. The center of who I am is found in everything He is.

This is so important to the restoration of the withered soul because there are so many different areas which attempt to define a person. A person's job, friends, spouse, hobbies and abilities will all try to define him. The message of the Gospel is that you are no longer defined by anything other than Christ in you. He is literally your life.

My favorite statement of all the above is "Christ is fused to my spirit." The word *fusion* means *the merging of diverse elements into a unified whole for the purpose of power.* When a person makes coffee, he takes two diverse elements, water and coffee, and forces them together. When a person takes hot water and coffee and mixes them together, he gets coffee. No one has ever mixed hot water and coffee and received nice, pure water. No, the two substances fuse. One rule of fusion is that the strongest substance wins. For example, water and coffee always make coffee. Coffee wins! When Christ and my life fused together, the strongest Person won. My life is no longer defined by me, my behavior, my attitudes or my thoughts. My life is now defined by Him, His behavior, His attitudes and His thoughts.

If all this is true, how can someone reflect a completely opposite image? The answer is partially found in the coffee illustration. The used gym sock does not change the substance of the coffee, but it changes the flavor. There are many instances in our lives where our substance does not change, but our flavor does. We cannot separate Christ from our spirit[10], but we can put a dirty sock in it.

You exist in a body

There is an incredible dichotomy that every person in history has dealt with. Will I allow myself to be defined by my flesh or by my spirit? In Romans 7, the Apostle Paul talked about this being a huge struggle in his life. Our spirit is who we really are, but our body is what everyone including ourselves sees. There is a dichotomy between His gifts and our talents; between His righteousness and our religion; between His holiness and our works, between His thoughts and our thoughts, between His knowledge and our five senses.

Chapter Two

This war exists between our natural man and our spiritual man. The Bible says that they do not understand each other[11].

> *"The man without the Spirit [natural man] does not accept the things that come from the Spirit of God, for they are foolishness to him, and he cannot understand them, because they are spiritually discerned. The spiritual man [our spirit being] makes judgments about all things, but he himself is not subject to any man's judgment: "For who has known the mind of the Lord that he may instruct him?" But we have the mind of Christ."*

We have been taught that the natural man is an unsaved man, but this is not entirely true. What Paul is saying is that the natural side of us does not understand the things of the spirit. This is all too true. The natural man does not understand that in order to truly live, a person has to die. The flesh does not understand that to be first, you have to be last. The flesh does not understand that to receive, you have to give. This is entirely foreign to a system that wants its own desires here, now, today. Our body will constantly remind us of things that are not true in our spirit. For example, the body will carry the weight of guilt, illness, insecurity, pride, etc... However, our spirit contains our innocence, healing, confidence and humility. Remember, the spirit is not subject to any man's judgment. However, we take the judgments of men and take them on as the defining substance of our being. There are incredible mandates in scripture to live out of our spirit instead of our flesh. Here are a few of those statements —"Live in the spirit[12]"; "Keep step with the spirit[13]"; "Walk in the spirit[14]"; "Pray in the spirit[15]"; "Sing in the spirit[16]"; "Be led by the spirit[17]"; and "Minister the spirit[18]". We have many mandates to live out of the truth in our spirit. In other words, live out of God. However, the reality of life leads us oftentimes in other directions. Who or what decides which one we live out of?

You have a soul

The x-factor in defining our being is our soul. The soul contains the mind, will and emotions of a person. This entity is normally the deciding factor as to which side of the dichotomy we will let define us. How does this work? David in Psalm 39:3 said, "My heart grew hot within me, and as I meditated the fire burned, and then I spoke with my mouth." David is on to something that is true of his life and every person's life before or since. We are all unique. We all have different gifts, passions, personalities, experiences and abilities. However, we all respond and act in the same order. We think it, feel it, say it and do it in that order. Every behavior has a thought attached to it. Every thought has a feeling attached to it. Every feeling has a word attached to it. When you put the three together, it explains every behavior we will ever engage in.

Has anyone ever told you, "Do not live by your feelings."? I think people who say this are well-intentioned, and I do understand what they mean. They mean that someone should not make decisions based on feelings that are **not based on truth**. However, everything we do is based on feelings. How many times have you asked someone why they did something, and their response was, "Just because I felt like it."? Our soul chooses to feel the feelings of the flesh which lead to the deeds of the flesh, or our soul chooses to feel the feelings of the spirit which lead to the deeds of the spirit. To instruct someone to never live by their feelings is giving them an impossible task. It is like telling someone to quit thinking. Every thought has an emotion attached to it. This is why we choose not to think about some thoughts, and we choose to dwell on others.

For example, we have all heard thoughts on the news that evoke feelings. Sometimes those feelings get so intense that we yell at an inanimate television set as if they could hear us. Here is yet another example. Wherever you are right now as you are reading this book, stop and think about a person you love with all of your heart. I am talking about the person who means so much to you that it is beyond words. Think about them. What do they look like, smell like, act like, etc...? Now come back to the book. What feelings are you having right now? Those feelings are associated with thoughts. Our thoughts control our feelings.

On the other hand, we have all flipped through television channels to see starving and abused children. What do we do? Sometimes we call and try to help, but we always turn the channel. We do not want to dwell on thoughts that evoke horrible feelings.

One final example, if you saw the Passion of the Christ movie, then you experienced what I am talking about in totality. This is a movie with no spoken English. It was simply image after image that evoked thoughts. Those thoughts quickly turned to intense feelings which found people whispering prayers under their breath in the theater. Prayers like, "I'm so sorry, Lord. Please forgive me for doing that to You."; "I'm so sorry that they treated You that way." Do you see the pattern in every instance? We think it, feel it, say it and do it in that order.

Our soul finds itself in an epic struggle to choose between the feelings out of spirit versus the feelings out of flesh. This choice centers on our thoughts. Will we choose to think truth thoughts out of our spirit, or will we submit to the thoughts originating in our flesh? What could happen to our soul if we trained ourselves to think, "I am innocent because the blood of Christ has cleansed me from all my sin."? Is this thought true? Of course it is. What if we could feel the truth of that thought everyday? What would it feel like if I could feel totally innocent before God?

Why is it, though, that we have been entrusted with a truth as powerful as this, yet we choose to think that we are guilty because of something we did? We act as if the blood of Christ cleanses everyone else from their sin, but it is not powerful enough to cover our big mistakes. This is just one example of the wrestling match between the spirit and flesh where the soul has to cast the deciding vote. The soul is caught in the middle asking questions: "Which one will I think about?"; "Which one will I meditate on?"; Which one will I feel the truth of?" When the spirit wins that battle, our soul's health takes care of itself. The soul will feel the feelings of truth. Our behavior will follow, which will reinforce truth. This reinforcement will perpetuate more feelings of truth. That is the cycle we want to find ourselves in. Perpetual feelings of innocence, acceptance, confidence, mercy, love, peace, gentleness and so on. On the other hand, when our soul chooses to dwell on the thoughts of the flesh, perpetual guilt, anger, doubt, insecurity, self-consciousness and chaos ensue. These perpetual feelings cause a slow decay of the quality of our thoughts, feelings and decisions. Slowly but surely, our soul withers from something that has been given perpetual life by grace through faith to something that is defined by a conglomeration of self.

The good news that God restores our soul is found in the fact that we are defined by God. God sees Christ in us. If we can train ourselves to see that and set our minds on it, then our soul will begin the process of restoration. This is a process. We have years of training in how to think from the flesh. We do not have to try to be self-conscious, guilty, afraid or angry. However, by the blood of Christ, we can replace those thoughts and feelings with the thoughts and feelings of our spirit. Deep down inside of us there is a fountain of life just waiting to spring forth and restore our withered soul.

Endnotes
1. Matthew 7:1-7
2. Genesis 1:26; John 4:24
3. Colossians 1:27
4. Galatians 2:20
5. Colossians 3:3
6. Colossians 3:4
7. 1 Corinthians 6:17
8. Galatians 6
9. Exodus 34:6,7
10. Romans 8:38,39
11. 1 Corinthians 2:14
12. Galatians 5:16
13. Galatians 5:25
14. Galatians 5:16
15. Ephesians 6:18
16. 1 Corinthians 14:15
17. Galatians 5:18
18. Galatians 3:5

Why is My Soul Sagging?

When I was in high school and college, I was under the delusion that many people live under at that stage of life. I could eat or drink anything and did not have to worry about gaining weight or increasing the rate at which I appeared to age. I am sure that at some point we have all been there, so we never really become motivated to change our habits. We continually eat what we want, when we want and how we want. One day, out of the blue, with no warning, we wake up twenty-five pounds heavier than when we went to bed the night before. We look in the mirror to find wrinkles that we swear were not there yesterday. All of a sudden, reality hits and we realize that we are sagging! We are not nearly as good looking as we once thought we were. We do not feel as good as we once did.

Do you remember 'all nighters' in college? To try to pull that off now would place us in a coma for a week. We are sagging! Our energy is not as good. Our memories are not as sharp. It seems like, as far as our bodies are concerned, nothing is in the right place. We are sagging! We start to find excess skin. We look in the mirror one morning only to find a three inch hair coming off of our shoulder. Where did that come from? It was not there the night before. The three inch hair bolsters our curiosity, and we begin to examine our body. There is now hair on our back, coming out our nose, and, worst of all, in our ears. We are sagging!

The state of our souls can sag just as quickly. Statistically, depression is more rampant today than ever before. Women are twice as likely as men to be depressed while men are twice as likely to go undiagnosed. We have all had days where everything seemed to go right only to be ruined in a moment of our own or someone else's indiscretion. It seems like nothing is wrong with the world. Then, with almost no warning, a co-worker comments on our work ethic; our phone rings informing us of money we owe; we receive unexpected bad news of some sort; or an authority figure expresses disappointment with us. All of a sudden, our soul begins to side with the flesh. We believe things that we would never believe when things are going well. Thoughts like "I am no good"; "This is not going to work"; "I have no hope"; and "This is a disaster" fill our consciousness. Now our soul is firmly connected to a self-consciousness that leads to nothing. We now are moving down a road that leads to a place where our potential is defined by us instead of by God. It might only take one bump in the road to move our thoughts, feelings, words and behavior from God-awareness to self-awareness. This is why people can sag. Does God give any remedy for this in scripture?

In 2 Samuel 9:1-13, the Bible tells an incredible story of a man named Mephibosheth, King Saul's grandson through his son Jonathan. Here is the Biblical account:

> *David asked, "Is there anyone still left of the house of Saul to whom I can show kindness for Jonathan's sake?" Now there was a servant of Saul's household named Ziba. They called him to appear before David, and the king said to him, "Are you Ziba?" "Your servant," he replied. The king asked, "Is there no one still left of the house of Saul to whom I can show God's kindness?" Ziba answered the king, "There is still a son of Jonathan; he is crippled in both feet." "Where is he?" the king asked. Ziba answered, "He is at the*

*house of Makir son of Ammiel in Lo Debar." So King David had him brought from Lo Debar, from the house of Makir son of Ammiel. When Mephibosheth son of Jonathan, the son of Saul, came to David, he bowed down to pay him honor. David said, "Mephibosheth!" "Your servant," he replied. "Don't be afraid," David said to him, "for I will surely show you kindness for the sake of your father Jonathan. I will restore to you all the land that belonged to your grandfather Saul, and you will always eat at my table." Mephibosheth bowed down and said, **"What is your servant, that you should notice a dead dog like me?"** Then the king summoned Ziba, Saul's servant, and said to him, "I have given your master's grandson everything that belonged to Saul and his family. You and your sons and your servants are to farm the land for him and bring in the crops, so that your master's grandson may be provided for. And Mephibosheth, grandson of your master, will always eat at my table." (Now Ziba had fifteen sons and twenty servants.) Then Ziba said to the king, "Your servant will do whatever my lord the king commands his servant to do." So Mephibosheth ate at David's table like one of the king's sons. Mephibosheth had a young son named Mica, and all the members of Ziba's household were servants of Mephibosheth. And Mephibosheth lived in Jerusalem, because he always ate at the king's table, and he was crippled in both feet.*

Chapter Three

We lack understanding of covenant

Years before this happened David made a blood covenant with Jonathan. The Hebrew blood covenant was a seven-step process that helps explain much of this passage and gives us particular insight into our own relationship with our King. A Hebrew covenant was called a *barit*. The word literally meant to cut. If two people in Israel wanted to cut covenant with each other, they would come together in front of witnesses and declare their intent to cut a covenant. The seven-step process would begin.

Firstly, they would trade coats. This represented everything of a person's life coming on another. Everything on David's life is now on Jonathan, and everything on Jonathan's life is now on David. This imagery exists in many different places in the Bible. One example is when Elijah chose Elisha as his successor by placing his coat on him. In our relationship with God, all of Christ is placed on us for the Bible says that we are "clothed with Christ[1]." Likewise, all of our life is placed on Him at the cross for the Bible declares that He bore all our sin, suffering, sickness and shame. We now have an exchanged life where we do not live out of our coat, but out of His.

Secondly, they would trade belts. Today, a belt is a fashion statement that should match our shoes in a fashion utopia. In David's day, the belt represented all the resources a person had at their disposal for protection. It held their weapons. So David would have vowed everything at his disposal to protect Jonathan, and Jonathan would have made the same vow to David. The implications for this passage as well as our life are so awesome. God has vowed everything at His disposal for protection to us, and we vow everything at our disposal to protect Him. He has promised His providence of protection. That is why the Bible teaches that no weapons formed against us will prosper[2]. They can't!! Anything that dares come against you must first go through everything God has at His disposal for protection.

Thirdly, they would sacrifice an animal by splitting it down the middle. This would seal the deal in blood. The pool of blood would mix between them. They would then lock arms and walk in a figure eight motion around the blood of sacrifice. 'Eight' in Hebrew culture is the number of new beginnings. In other words, because of the blood of the sacrifice, every part of the person's life before the covenant is gone. It is as if it did not even exist. Everything is now made new. David and Jonathan's life would be divided between before covenant and after covenant. The same is true of our life. Our life before the covenant is completely gone. Every sin, every mistake, every sickness, every disappointment and every righteous act are all gone. We get to start completely over with God. All the old things are passed away, and everything has been made new[3].

Fourthly, they would read all the blessings and curses of Deuteronomy 28. Have you ever read this? This is an incredibly exhaustive list of blessings and curses. You might have read the above passage and wondered why David would care about anyone in Saul's family because Saul had tried to kill David for years. The reason is covenant. If David breaks his covenant with Jonathan, then all the curses of Deuteronomy 28 will be loosed on him. The same is true with our relationship with God. God cannot break His covenant with us. The same rules apply because He is just. If you are anything like me, then this is scary because we break our side all the time. Does that mean the curses are loosed on us? NO!! The truth is that the *barit* between us and God is not between us and God.

Hebrews 8 says that God knew that man could not keep his side of the deal, so, therefore, He would always find fault with man. God's solution to this problem was to place Himself in our spirit as a seal of redemption and then make a covenant with Himself. That is why the Bible declares that since God could swear by no greater, He swore by Himself[4]. Our covenant with God is as secure as the name of God itself. He swore by His own name. In 2 Timothy 2:12,13, Paul declares that "If we disown Him, then He will disown us, but if we become unfaithful, He will remain faithful to us because He cannot disown Himself." God has decided before the witnesses in Heaven to cut a *barit* with us. That is one awesome place to be.

Fifthly, they would cut their hands and clasp them together so that the blood would mingle down their arms and mix with the blood of the sacrifice. This was a second sealing of the covenant in blood. The issue was to make a mark that would make it obvious that a person was in covenant. If someone cut themselves down the center of their hand, it would leave a pretty serious scar. This scar became a sign or a mark of covenant. Therefore, if someone decided to attack David, they would have seen the sign of covenant and would have known that he was not alone. The same would have been true of Jonathan as well. Our relationship with God is the same way. Both God and I have a mark. The Bible says that my name is written on His hand, and His name is the circumcision of my heart. In other words, when the accuser of our soul attacks us to Jesus, Jesus looks at His hand. He sees our name, and knows He is in covenant. He basically tells the devil to 'talk to the hand'.

Sixthly, they would trade sir names. This is very similar to power of attorney. David would have taken on Jonathan's name and all the authority that came with it. Likewise, Jonathan would have taken on David's name and all the authority that came with it. Either one could sign legal documents, checks, contracts or purchase orders. Imagine the implications for our life with God. We have the right to pray 'in Jesus' name'. Jesus said, "Anything you ask in my name, you will have." What gives us the right to access the name? What gives us the right to the character, authority, and environment of God? The answer is covenant.

Seventhly, they would feed each other bread. David would have fed Jonathan bread, and vice versa. This symbolized all of a person's life going into the other. All of David is now in Jonathan. They are inseparable. Paul said that nothing could separate us from the love of God in Christ Jesus[5]. How is that possible? The reason is that He is in me. IN!!! He has fused Himself to me[6]. *Fusion* means *the merging of diverse elements into a unified whole for the purpose of power*. For example, when you merge tea and hot water, you get tea. The tea leaves and water have merged into a unified whole, and once tea is made, the two cannot be separated. Also, the strongest substance wins. You never combine tea and water and get water. The same is true with my relationship with God. I am no longer me, but I am Christ in me. In other words, my elements and Christ's elements merge into a unified whole for the purpose of power. WOW! What a wonderful God.

To increase our knowledge of covenant makes us more aware of our standing, possessions, position and resources of our place with God. This goes a long way in determining what our soul will become aware of and attach itself to. This determines what we live out of — our eternal spirit or our temporal body. A correct understanding of covenant is a key in the cure for the sagging soul.

We get to the place of no bread

This story is so full of implications for life that we have to look at it in levels. On the surface, there is a pretty amazing chronology of events that take place. In the chaos of the house of Saul falling, a nurse picks up one of the grandchildren, Mephibosheth, and attempts to run with him in order to get him to safety. In the process, she trips and falls on the boy. Consequently, he is left with crippled feet. She hides him in the house of Achir, who is the son of Ammiel, in Lo Debar. The reason for this is that, under normal circumstances, David would have killed everyone who was still in Saul's household to avoid a possible heir to the throne causing a revolution. At the very least, if you were lucky, they would just castrate you. Who wants to be the lucky one? Just kill me.

David eventually finds him, and, instead of killing him, takes him into his house as a part of royalty. He gives him servants, restores his land and lets him eat at his table for the rest of his life. This is all in spite of the fact that he is crippled.

Is there a deeper meaning in this passage besides the facts surrounding covenant and the natural chronology of events? The first thing I want to point out is Mephibosheth's self-description as a 'dead dog'. We have to realize that Mephibosheth was told that if David ever found him, David would kill or castrate him. Family affirmations play such a big role in our lives. The words parents speak release certain feelings which create expectations to rule us. The expectations become the filter for how we interpret our environments. When Mephibosheth heard the stomping of David's horses coming for him, fear gripped him. He would have thought that the king wanted nothing to do with him except to harm him. The same is true for us. Some have been taught that if God finds us, He will kill or hurt us. God is mad!! We even sing songs that confess it. For instance, the old song "At the Cross" has a line in it that defines us as a 'worm'. That is pretty close on the social ladder to a 'dead dog'. Consequently, we relate to God as if we were a 'dead dog' instead of a son of the King. This makes us more self-absorbed which results in sagging even worse. This perpetual cycle is something we definitely want to avoid. We can not relate to God as a dead dog and expect to experience the rights of sons.

The second thing I want to point out is that he was taken from his destiny to a place called Lo Debar. The name Lo Debar means the land of no bread. On the surface, Lo Debar is a place of lack; a wilderness of some sort where resources are limited. Looking deeper, there is spiritual significance behind the imagery of bread.

There is a continual allusion in the Bible to bread being the Word of God. The Bible says that man does not live by bread alone, but by every word that proceeds out of the mouth of God[7]. Jesus uses this quotation from the Torah to fend off the temptation of Satan. Later, Jesus teaches the disciples how to pray by saying, "Give us this day, our daily bread[8]." What was He talking about?

Every day the children of Israel would have to go out and gather manna for the day. They would gather manna each day for six days. On the sixth day, they were allowed to gather a double portion because the Sabbath day was coming. On the

Sabbath day, the priest would prepare the showbread for the twelve tribes of Israel. In the tabernacle, the showbread was in the inner court, and the manna was in the Holy of Holies. The Holy of Holies is symbolic of the spirit of a man while the inner court was symbolic of the soul. The imagery is pretty awesome. The manna was their 'daily bread'. It is symbolic of God's Word. As we get our daily Word, it creates a place in our spirit where that Word does not rot. It prepares our heart for the serving of the showbread from our pastor once a week. The manna makes the showbread meaningful.

In other words, Mephibosheth is stuck in the land of no bread which means he is stuck in the land of no Word. He was in a place that had no words of hope, no words of love, no words of inspiration, no words of motivation, no words of healing. It is a land of no Word. Sometimes we get to places of lack and wilderness, and in that wilderness God seems as if He has become a deaf mute. He is not listening, and He is not speaking. In this environment, we become crippled. There seems to be nothing we can do. The only way out is for our King to show up and take us to His house and give us bread. We need a fresh word from Him and not from anyone else. No one else can save the situation except the King. The good news is that our King is on the way. He is coming not to do you harm, but to give you a hope and a future.[9]

David's downfall started in Lo Debar as well. Two chapters later, David commits adultery and murder. Where did it all start? Scholars tell us that Ammiel was Bathsheba's father, so David went to Bathsheba's family's house in order to rescue Mephibosheth. Is there any way that this was the start of his infatuation with Bathsheba? Maybe Mephibosheth's place of 'no

Word' crippled him, but when David entered the place of 'no Word' it attached his eyes to someone who was not his. We will always fill our void for daily bread with something that our eyes attach to. This will quickly send our soul into a withered state. Why? Nothing can take the place of our daily bread. We cannot fill it with anything else. We have to eat at our King's table daily for that is what He desires[10].

The third facet of this passage I want you to notice is the emphasis on his crippled feet. Why would they make such a big deal of this? In Hebraic culture, a person is either in a state of *tamei* or *tahor*. The word *tamei* means *unclean*, so a leper would have to walk through town screaming *tamei, tamei, tamei*. The word *tahor* means *clean*. Any physical blemish made someone *tamei*. If someone was *tamei* or touched someone who was *tamei*, then they could not enter into the temple. That is why the crippled people would lie at the temple gate. It was as close as they could get to the presence of God while being in a state of *tamei*.

Remember the story of the paralyzed man who they lowered through the roof by his mat? The reason they used a mat was because they could not touch him or they too would be *tamei*. Jesus reaches down and **touches** him, and the man walked. In other words, the very thing that made him *tamei* became *tahor*. God is in the business of calling things *tahor* that are in a state of *tamei*. He loves it. Do you realize that if the crippled man was not healed, then Jesus would have been considered *tamei*?

This message of the Gospel rings true throughout this story of Mephibosheth. He is ceremonially and permanently unclean, yet David gives him all his land and lets him eat at his table. This man in a permanent state of *tamei* is allowed at the king's table. That is the message of the Gospel, and one that restores the soul. Our soul might be withered; our body might be ill; we might have sinned; our place is in Lo Debar; but God is standing to restore our soul. He is coming to take us back to our place of destiny. He is standing before us declaring us *tahor*. Clean in His sight. We can eat at His table and allow Him to restore us from a state of *tamei* to a state of *tahor*.

Listen to the heart of God. Can you hear Him? He is saying you are His child. It does not matter what your family told you about Him. It does not matter how you measure up to everyone else. He is inviting you to His table, crippled feet and all. He is waiting to wrap you in His ever-loving arms and restore your soul. He is longing to unlock from inside of you a wellspring of life that will flow to the world around you, so that everyone will know that He is God.

Endnotes
1. Colossians 3
2. Isaiah 54:17
3. 2 Corinthians 5:17
4. Hebrews 6:13
5. Romans 8:38,39
6. 1 Corinthians 6:17
7. Deuteronomy 8:3
8. Matthew 6:11
9. Jeremiah 29:11
10. Revelation 3:20

How Can I Live From Friday to Sunday?

SOMEONE KNOCKED ON MY OFFICE DOOR. When I answered the door, something came over me. I knew as soon as I opened the door that the course of my day was going to change.

On the other side of my office door was a lady sobbing very hard. It was one of those cries that come straight from the gut. She was very pregnant and holding the hand of a two-year-old. I asked her to come in and have a seat. I tried to calm her down. She told me that her husband had left her eight months pregnant and with a two-year-old at home. She had no job, and no way to support herself. She looked at me through these huge tears and asked me to help her.

At that point, I realized that all of my seminary training did not prepare me for everything. Some things just have to be learned by experience. What do you say to someone in that situation? What can you say? What don't you say? This was very awkward. I invited her in and listened to her for a couple of hours. I provided direction to her for friendship, accountability and support. The good news is that her story ends well. She made it through that season, and God gave her a new job, husband and family. However, the question still remains. How do you live through a time when it looks like all your dreams have crashed into the ground?

The disciples went through something very similar. We have to put the last few hours of Jesus' life in context of the bigger story. They were not just twelve fishermen who Jesus chose. Rather, they were twelve men given a complete second chance by Jesus. In Hebraic culture, children were required to memorize up to the end of Leviticus by age six and the entire Torah by age twelve. Somewhere between ten years of age and twelve years of age the religious authorities would decide whether or not a child was a candidate to go through Rabbinical training. If a child was deemed worthy to go through this, then they would continue on with their training. This would require them to be placed under the mentorship of a Rabbi who the child would follow until his Rabbinical ministry started. If a child was not deemed worthy, then they were sent back to work in their family business and were disqualified from the highest honor for a Jewish person, which was being a Rabbi.

Therefore, when Jesus approached twelve fishermen, He was approaching twelve people who were disqualified from ministry several years before. Get the picture! Twelve fishermen are doing what they have done for years, and a Rabbi shows up and asks them to follow Him. They immediately dropped their nets and followed. Why? It was a second chance for them. These twelve men had been disqualified from the honor of following a Rabbi, and, in one moment, a Rabbi gives them a second chance at ministry. The twelve drop everything; jobs, family, children, success and position. This sacrifice was all for a chance to be restored into the ministry of God. They placed all their hopes and dreams in this one Rabbi because He was the only one giving them a chance. Over the journey of getting to know Him, they realize that this is no ordinary Rabbi. This is the One. This is the Messiah who they had read about as children. This is the One the hopes and dreams of Israel as a nation rested on. How would they ever be free from Roman rule? Would the kingdom of Messiah ever be established? All of their hopes, all of their dreams, everything is found in this one Man.

One Friday, this all changed. He had told them this day was coming, but they did not believe Him. He predicted His own suffering, death and resurrection. Then He pulled it off, but they never understood what He was talking about. They could not conceive that the Rabbi who rescued them and gave them a second chance would be killed. They could not imagine how the Messiah could possibly die. The Messiah was supposed to establish the kingdom. Can you imagine their thoughts? Surely, when the Romans arrested Him, they watched from a distance thinking, "When will He make His move?" He did not. They beat Him with a beating that killed seven out of ten people. He did not make His move. They put a crown of thorns on His head. Maybe now He would make His move? No. They made Him walk a cross up a hill for His own execution. He did not make His move. They nailed Him to the cross and raised Him up for all to see. He still did not make His move. They watched Him die.

In their minds, Messiahs did not die. They watched all their hopes, dreams, aspirations and visions die that Friday afternoon. Can you imagine what was going on inside? Everything that meant anything to them died. Everything!!! There was no hope, and they had no idea that Sunday was on the way. Remember, every time Jesus taught on the resurrection, the Bible said that they did not understand Him. This had to have been the greatest moment of despair ever recorded. How did they live from Friday to Sunday without knowing what Sunday would hold? How did they make it through the uncertainty? How did they make it through the depression, the shame, the guilt and the gut-level agony? They did not know what Sunday would entail.

Anatomy of the withered soul

What happens to our soul when we find ourselves living from Friday to Sunday? Our soul will always feel something.

We cannot avoid that. Our soul will either attach itself to the spirit feelings or to our natural feelings. Using the disciples' experience as a case study, what does a withered soul look like? What happens to our soul in times like they faced from Friday to Sunday?

Fear

> *"On the evening of that first day of the week, when the disciples were together, **with the doors locked for fear of the Jews**, Jesus came and stood among them and said, "Peace be with you!"*
>
> *-- John 20:19*

One of the things the disciples faced from Friday to Sunday is fear. Any time we witness our dreams die in a moment, fear naturally follows. This is the part of us that always plays out the worst case scenario to the tenth power. One definition of fear that I have seen is: <u>F</u>alse, <u>E</u>ducation, <u>A</u>ppearing, <u>R</u>eal. This really encapsulates the problem of fear. A lie that appears so real gets into us so that we feel it. Our soul attaches to that lie and we begin to live out of it as if it were true. We feel the lie to the point that the lie determines our behavior. It determined the disciples' behavior. Eleven of the mightiest men of faith who have ever lived found themselves locked in an attic. What is going on? They are hiding from the same people that they would find themselves preaching to in just forty days. Forty days from that moment these same people would find themselves rebuking the same people they were hiding from. Peter tells them "**YOU** killed Him with the help of evil men[1]." Amazing!

He was just hiding from them. What changed? Did the facts change? NO!! His knowledge of the facts changed. His perception of reality changed. His dream walked back in the room; the dream he saw die. Remember, he **saw** his dream die. There is no argument with what you see. He just knew there was no hope for his dream. He saw Him die. Fear ensued. His false education appeared real. Now, however, the perception of the facts changed. He is completely aware that his dream is alive. His dream walked out of the grave and into the upper room. Now the false education appears to be false instead of real. All of a sudden, the truth comes forth instead of the lie. The lie put Peter in a locked room. The truth placed him preaching to thousands. When we become afraid, it is most often due to some lie appearing as truth. This can force us to abandon our dreams, lock ourselves in a room, and hope for the best. It is almost a state of learned helplessness. We see no way out because we saw our dream die. What gives us liberty from the locked room of fear is a knowledge of the truth.

Guilt

> *When they had finished eating, Jesus said to Simon Peter, "Simon son of John, do you truly love me more than these?" "Yes, Lord," he said, "you know that I love you." Jesus said, "Feed my lambs." Again Jesus said, "Simon son of John, do you truly love me?" He answered, "Yes, Lord, you know that I love you." Jesus said, "Take care of my sheep." The third time he said to him, "Simon son of John, do you love me?" Peter was hurt because Jesus asked him the third time, "Do you love me?"*

Chapter Four

He said, "Lord, you know all things; you know that I love you." Jesus said, "Feed my sheep."

-- John 21:15-17

This is an incredible encounter between Peter and Jesus considering the context. Just a few days before, Peter had cursed and denied Him three times. He turned his back on his dream and eventually watched Him die. Can you imagine the guilt he must have felt? What kind of thoughts had to be going through his mind on his bed at night? That feeling of weight on your chest that is almost unbearable? That feeling where you are convinced that you are condemned forever? For days he had felt this. There had to be a point where it was almost unbearable. It had to be. He completely gave his hopes, dreams and the most important Person in his life over to the enemy. The guilt had to be unbelievable. When things happen to us that we do not deserve nor understand, guilt is a natural by-product. It is natural for us to blame ourselves. God's plan was being implemented all along, but Peter did not know it.

That is the context for which we witness this encounter between Peter and Jesus. What would Jesus say? What would Jesus do? Remember, Peter was disqualified from carrying on a Rabbi's teaching way back at the age of ten. Would he be disqualified again? Would the Rabbi that gave him his second chance turn on him? Common sense would dictate that Jesus would have every right to react however He saw fit. When the encounter takes place, Peter had to be in amazement of Jesus' response. He simply asked three times if Peter loved Him. Three in Hebraic numerology is the number of complete witness. In other words, Jesus wanted a complete witness that Peter was in love with Him. Peter had probably played a conversation in his imagination with Jesus many times over the previous few days. What would he say to Jesus if he ever saw Him again? Now is the chance, and all Jesus wants to know is if Peter loves Him.

Notice the restoration method of Jesus. Jesus did not ask him if he was sorry. He did not make him grovel, moan, weep and wail at an altar. He did not even bring up the sin. There was no huge confrontation, so that Peter could become broken. There was not a long time span of 'sabbatical from ministry' so that he could get his heart right. Jesus asked one question, "Do you love me?" What a relief that must have been for Peter. He had already considered the reality that his life of carrying the Rabbi's message was over when grace walked down the beach that day and cooked him breakfast. Jesus was only concerned with one thing, "Do you love me?" This was the one area that Peter was sure of. He knew he loved Christ with all of his heart. Get the picture! Christ reinstated Peter to ministry with Him only a few days after the most blatant denial ever recorded.

Maybe God allowed this to be recorded in the Gospels for us. It is not so much about Peter and Jesus on a beach, but rather it is about us and Jesus in our life. We feel like we have failed Him miserably. We feel like we will be disqualified from our dream, our hope, our calling. We wonder what He is thinking. We need to hear Jesus' words loud and clear. "DO YOU LOVE ME?" Allow the sentiments of that to wrap you in His love. Allow His heart for Peter to penetrate your heart. We are not hopeless failures. We are not doomed to lives we have always known. NO. Our Lord is waiting for us on a beach with breakfast in hand. Do we love Him? Inside that question is the answer to the restoration of our souls because the answer carries a promise that He will wipe our sins out and remember them no more[2].

Anger

> "I told you that I am he," Jesus answered. "If you are looking for me, then let these men go." This happened so that the words he had spoken would be fulfilled: "I have not lost one of those you gave me." Then Simon Peter, who had a sword, drew it and struck the high priest's servant, cutting off his right ear. (The servant's name was Malchus.) Jesus commanded Peter, "Put your sword away! Shall I not drink the cup the Father has given me?"
>
> -- John 18:8-11

When things happen that we do not deserve nor do we understand, anger oftentimes ensues. Anger is a dangerous thing because it is secondary. People do not just get mad. Something is triggering it. Anger does crazy things to us. Look at what it did to Peter. He assaulted a member of the High Priest's staff. What was he thinking? If Jesus did not intervene, Peter might have been killed right next to Jesus. Peter's anger got the best of his reasoning skills. This happens to us. One study suggests that a person can lose 25% of their IQ when they get into a state of heightened anger. Most people cannot afford that. To lose 25% of our IQ places most people into a borderline mentally handicapped state. Think about it. When is the last time you made a wise decision in the middle of an angry moment?

Sometimes the anger gets us so worked up that we cannot even string together consecutive intelligent words. Men grunt, growl or string together a conglomeration of unintelligible words. Why? The blood from our brain has rushed to our major muscle groups to prepare for a fight. We cannot make an intelligent decision.

One problem we encounter from Friday to Sunday is that the events get filtered through anger. We do not necessarily see all the facts. Jesus reminds Peter that He has to go through with the will of the Father. Peter's anger was no different from ours. It skewed the situation. We make decisions that we have to live with based on a skewed view of reality. This begins a process of unhealthy emotions that only validate the skewed reality. Without warning, the withered soul is saturated with feelings of anger.

God wants to restore our souls to peace. The chaos that comes with living from Friday to Sunday leaves us in a seemingly hopeless place. He is telling us that He is in control. The anger is getting us nowhere. The God of all peace is standing before us offering us His peace. His peace surpasses all understanding. His peace surpasses all misunderstanding. No matter what our situation is, God is offering us something that surpasses our knowledge of our situation. It is completely God.

Doubt and Isolation

> *Now Thomas (called Didymus), one of the Twelve, was not with the disciples when Jesus came. So the other disciples told him, "We have seen the Lord!" But he said to them, "Unless I see the nail marks in his hands and put my finger where the nails*

Chapter Four

were, and put my hand into his side, I will not believe it." A week later his disciples were in the house again, and Thomas was with them. Though the doors were locked, Jesus came and stood among them and said, "Peace be with you!" Then he said to Thomas, "Put your finger here; see my hands. Reach out your hand and put it into my side. Stop doubting and believe." Thomas said to him, "My Lord and my God!"

-- John 20:24-28

When Friday to Sunday moments happen, our confidence gets shaken to the core of who we are. It happened to Thomas. I personally feel Thomas has a bad rap. Every person in Sunday School learns to attribute the person of Thomas with the adjective 'doubting'. He has been called 'doubting Thomas' for generations. Is that really fair? The Bible says that he was not there when Jesus first appeared to the others. In reality, he was the only one not hiding in a locked attic, and he is the one generations of people have learned to call 'doubting'. Just a thought, but maybe he was the most 'together' of all of them.

The mistake he made was to isolate from all the people he had community with. He had spent the previous three-and-a-half years with this group. When the group's dream died, he isolated. He basically needed his space. He had given up on the pursuit that this incredible group of people followed. We do the same thing. When it looks like the ship is sinking, we isolate. We separate ourselves from the very people who breathed life into us for years. We isolate.

Plus, can you really blame him for not being eager to jump back on the Messiah bandwagon? He had just given three-and-a-half years of his life to a dream of Messiah. He watched his hopes, dreams and aspirations die as well. Three days later the same people claim that they have seen the Messiah. Thomas simply proclaims in a witty way that he needs to see what they had already seen. If James had been the one missing, I am sure that we would be saying 'doubting James' instead of 'doubting Thomas'.

We are the same way. When our dreams die, we need to see something different in order to combat the feeling that our dreams are dead. We need to touch our Lord. We do not need to hear about Him. We need to touch Him. We need to feel with our own fingers what He did for us. We need to feel how much He loves us. We need to feel the price He paid. In that moment comes a restoration command that breathes new life into our hopes, dreams and aspirations. Jesus looks at us just like He did Thomas and commands us to quit doubting and start believing. Hear the voice of God! Quit doubting! Quit scrutinizing everything! Quit being so self-conscious! Quit thinking of reasons why you can't, and begin to reach out and touch Him. He is standing with you. Touch Him!!! Allow Him to renew your vision. Allow Him to restore your belief in His dream for your life. In that heart is a moment of restoring our withered soul.

Settling for the familiar

Simon Peter, Thomas (called Didymus), Nathaniel from Cana in Galilee, the sons of Zebedee, and two other disciples were together. "I'm going out to fish," Simon Peter told them, and they said, "We'll go with you." So they went out and got into the boat, but that night they caught nothing.

-- John 21:2-3

The disciples had given their lives to carrying on the message and Torah interpretation of Messiah Jesus. When Jesus died, they thought their chance to carry the legacy of the Rabbi died with Him. What did they do? They went right back to the very thing that Jesus took them out of. Is there anything wrong with fishing? Absolutely not! That is not the point. The point is that they were willing to settle for fishing for fish when Jesus' plan was to make them fishers of men. That is the sin in it. Settling for being fishers of fish when God was screaming that He had a plan for them to be fishers of men was missing the mark.

How do we find ourselves willing to settle for less so easily? Many of us know what kind of plan God has for us. We have seen it, felt it, touched it, sensed it and experienced small parts of it. We know Jesus is saying that this is just a taste of what is to come. Peter would lead 3,000 people to Christ in 40 days, yet he was willing to settle for being a fisherman. It is so easy to rationalize. I can hear his reasoning with the other six with him: "What's wrong with fishing?" "We will make a good living." "We were happy before weren't we?" "Fishing is fun." "We know how to fish. It is our comfort zone." "Did Jesus ever really intend for us to be fishers of men? Think about it, He did all the work anyway. We were just along for the ride."

Settling for the familiar is common to Friday-to-Sunday moments. We shrink back into isolation and create an atmosphere of guilt, fear, anger and doubt. At this point, the only thing that eases the pain is to revert back to how we were and totally ignore the bigger calling. The bigger calling just died. There is no way we will ever be able to fulfill it, and we convince ourselves that the only way is to go back to fishing. The problem is that the old way does not have the same favor. Notice that the professional fisherman did not catch one fish. NOT ONE!! When God has a bigger calling, the familiar thing we are settling for will never satisfy us again.

The good news is that standing on the shoreline is the embodiment of their dream. He is just far enough for them to wonder. Friend, your dreams are closer than you think. Do not settle for the familiar and miss the fantastic. Do not settle for your life defined by you when your life can be defined by Him. Do not settle! Do not settle! Do not settle! Your King is standing on the beach with breakfast ready. His gifts and calling are without revoke. His plan has never changed. It is time for us to jump out of the boat of the familiar and into our destiny with Him. All it takes is one jump of faith. Do not stay in the boat of the familiar. Take the plunge. He stands ready to restore everything to you, and you too will be able to shout out, "He restores my soul."

Endnotes
1. Acts 2:23
2. Hebrews 8

The Resurrection Guarantee

I AM SO GLAD that many things in life are known to be temporary. Sometimes the only hope we have is that an end is coming. The examples are numerous. When I participated in high school athletics, the least favorite part was always the conditioning. Most of us loved to scrimmage and did not mind doing skill drills. However, the conditioning part was brutal especially in soccer. We would run wind sprints followed by a masochistic running exercise called a 'wagon train'. The only thing that allowed someone to mentally get through this exercise was to realize that the moment was temporary.

How about pregnancy and labor pains? If there was any sense that this period of time would never end, then women all over would slowly begin to lose their minds. My grandmother is quick to point out that giving birth was much harder in her day. As a matter of fact, she gave birth to my father at home with a midwife, and he weighed 13 pounds. Yikes! That is a fairly good sized watermelon birthing from inside your body. Plus, before the birth, there were 40 weeks of pregnancy complete with morning sickness, mood swings, cravings, hot flashes and vomiting. All this is true, yet women choose to get pregnant over and over again. The only explanation is that the joy from the birth far outweighs the pain of the season of pregnancy and labor.

Perspective is everything. Once we see a light at the end of the tunnel, we can live through almost anything that comes our way. In the previous chapter, we discussed what happens to the state of our soul when we are living from Friday to Sunday. What about the Sunday moment? What happens when our dream walks into the room? What happens when our hope is risen from the dead? When the light is seen at the end of the tunnel?

Chapter Five

Part of getting to this moment of victory is keeping an eternal perspective. Perspective is the key to focus. You cannot focus a camera lens properly without understanding the perspective of the shot you are trying to get. The same is true in life. Our perspective gets out of balance and causes our focus to be off-center. At that point, all of life is a blur, and we cannot seem to make sense of anything. Sometimes all we need is a perspective change and everything else follows suit. We need to realize that our situation is temporary. It will end. There is a light at the end of the tunnel. You might point out that I do not know your situation. I just do not know how bad it is. You are right. I don't know or understand. I am truly sorry for whatever you are going through that causes you pain. However, listen to the situation the Apostle Paul found himself in:

> *"Are they servants of Christ? (I am out of my mind to talk like this.) I am more. I have worked much harder, been in prison more frequently, been flogged more severely, and been exposed to death again and again. Five times I received from the Jews the forty lashes minus one. Three times I was beaten with rods, once I was stoned, three times I was shipwrecked, I spent a night and a day in the open sea, I have been constantly on the move. I have been in danger from rivers, in danger from bandits, in danger from my own countrymen, in danger from Gentiles; in danger in the city, in danger in the country, in danger at sea; and in danger from false brothers. I have labored and toiled and have often gone without sleep; I have*

> *known hunger and thirst and have often gone without food; I have been cold and naked. Besides everything else, I face daily the pressure of my concern for all the churches. Who is weak, and I do not feel weak? Who is led into sin, and I do not inwardly burn?"*
>
> *-- 2 Corinthians 11:23-29*

Take a hard look at the list here that is making up Paul's situation. Without some context, it is easy to read over the list and not feel the situation. He says that he was beaten five times from the Jews with 39 lashes. This was a part of the Jewish justice system. They would take a 'cat-of-nine-tails' and hit a man with it 39 times because 40 would kill them. This whip had nine belts with steal tips with shards of loose metal and glass in the tip. If you saw the <u>Passion of the Christ</u>, you would have witnessed this phenomenon that Paul experienced on five separate occasions. How does your situation compare to that? He said that he had been beaten with rods on three different occasions. In other words, a group of huge men took big sticks and beat him all over his body until he fell unconscious.

He says that he was stoned once. We have to understand the intent here. If the Jewish authorities thought you were teaching heresy, they could take you to the edge of a fifteen foot cliff and tie your hands behind your back and shove you off the cliff. Hopefully you would die when you landed on your face. If you did not die, they would take turns throwing boulders down on your head until you died. The Jewish leaders tried this with Jesus once, but He got away. Paul did not. He experienced this and lived through it.

Chapter Five

He paints this picture that almost looks like a professional counseling session gone very bad. Feel what Paul is saying. He is almost coming across as having some sort of paranoid personality disorder. Look at the list. There is danger everywhere: in rivers, seas, land, Jews, Gentiles and false brothers. That pretty much covers things. He is tired, hungry, cold and naked. On top of all this, he is feeling the weight and pressure from being a pastor. This has taken him to a point where he is numb. He says that he is weak and yet cannot even feel it. He can be led into sin and not care. These are heavy statements. You compile all the above situations, and you will see a messed-up life. Everything is going wrong, yet he says that he is boasting about it. Not complaining, but boasting. How does that happen? How can someone take a Friday-to-Sunday season like this one and turn it into a positive?

The answer comes from his perspective. Look at how he describes his situation in two different scriptures:

> *"We put no stumbling block in anyone's path, so that our ministry will not be discredited. Rather, as servants of God we commend ourselves in every way: in great endurance; in troubles, hardships and distresses; in beatings, imprisonments and riots; in hard work, sleepless nights and hunger; in purity, understanding, patience and kindness; in the Holy Spirit and in sincere love; in truthful speech and in the power of God; with weapons of righteousness in the right hand and in the left; through glory and dishonor, bad report and*

good report; genuine, yet regarded as impostors; known, yet regarded as unknown; dying, and yet we live on; beaten, and yet not killed; sorrowful, yet always rejoicing; poor, yet making many rich; **_having nothing, and yet possessing everything._**"

--2 Corinthians 6:3-10

Notice the thought at the end. Is it really possible to have nothing and possess everything? How does that work? It is possible to have something and yet not really have it. Likewise, it is possible to not have something, and yet have it. Possession and ownership are two different things. For example, I have a friend who has an incredible $4,800 guitar. He can play, but he is not a pro. When my guitar professional friends come over and play his guitar, it sounds different. The friends do not possess the physical guitar, but they own and understand it more. The list is numerous. A person can have kids without being a good dad. He can have friends without being a good friend. This is so sad. Solomon said that he had everything and withheld no pleasure for himself, yet he owned nothing. At the same time, Paul is saying that he has nothing, yet he has everything. It is totally possible to be a part of the 'haves' and yet 'have not' and it is possible to have nothing and yet have life.

"*Therefore, since through God's mercy we have this ministry, we do not lose heart... But we have this treasure in jars of clay to show that this all-surpassing power is from God and not from us.*

Chapter Five

We are hard pressed on every side, but not crushed; perplexed, but not in despair; persecuted, but not abandoned; struck down, but not destroyed. We always carry around in our body the death of Jesus, so that the life of Jesus may also be revealed in our body. For we who are alive are always being given over to death for Jesus' sake, so that his life may be revealed in our mortal body. So then, death is at work in us, but life is at work in you. It is written: "I believed; therefore I have spoken." With that same spirit of faith we also believe and therefore speak, because we know that the one who raised the Lord Jesus from the dead will also raise us with Jesus and present us with you in his presence. All this is for your benefit, so that the grace that is reaching more and more people may cause thanksgiving to overflow to the glory of God. Therefore we do not lose heart. Though outwardly we are wasting away, yet inwardly we are being renewed day by day. **For our light and momentary troubles** *are achieving for us an eternal glory that far outweighs them all. So we fix our eyes not on what is seen, but on what is unseen. For what is seen is temporary, but what is unseen is eternal.*

--*2 Corinthians 4:1-18*

Look at Paul's amazing perspective on his life. Do not lose the context of the situation. All that he has gone through has not persuaded him to give up. The reason for his tenacity is that he knew he had a calling that was bigger than the problem. He says that God's mercy has given him a ministry, and that is why he will not give up. He uses this image of a clay pot's process of being finished. He is saying that sometimes being pressed is not a bad thing. Sometimes being crushed is simply part of the process. Sometimes being persecuted is necessary. This is amazing perspective.

Then he makes the most incredible comment of them all. He calls his life situation light and momentary. What? I can see where he might be able to convince himself that his trials are momentary, but there is absolutely no evidence that the trials are light. He has almost died on a regular basis at the hands of other men. This seems heavy, yet Paul says that they are light. What makes him come to this conclusion? He comes to this conclusion by defining the trials as temporary. If the trials are permanent, then there is nothing light about it. However, since the trials are temporary, then they are necessarily light because they will end. This perspective allowed him to focus on things that are eternal instead of temporal. Such a focus allowed him to always define himself by his eternal facets instead of his temporal.

Our Friday-to-Sunday seasons are light and momentary. They really are!!! The key to the resurrection moment is to see the light at the end of the tunnel. We have all experienced things that we thought were the end of the world as we know it only to laugh later at how crazy we were being. Call it what it is — light and momentary. The Bible declares that weeping will endure for a night, but joy comes in the morning[1]. Weeping is the strongest word you could possibly choose to use pertaining to crying. This person is so sad they are crying at a gut level.

The situation in their life is so hopeless that there seems to be no way out. Therefore, the weeping endures. To endure means to keep going. Have you ever met someone who it seems is never out of crisis? Their weeping is enduring. It is continual. Please hear the message of God to all who will listen.

The message is that your season has an end. Just as sure as night turns to day, that is how sure it is that your season will end. All nights turn to day. Every time!!! There is no exception. Night time turns to day time eventually. God is saying that He knows there is enduring weeping, but daybreak is coming. The night is momentary. When daybreak comes, we can either breakdown or breakthrough to our destiny. The season of weeping is coming to a close. Your season of joy is just beginning. The key is to not lose heart. In other words, do not give up!! Never, ever, ever, ever, ever, ever, ever give up!! God does not want a breakdown for us, but, rather, desires a breakthrough. Your resurrection Sunday is coming.

There are many things interconnected in the Bible. The message of this chapter is that the Sunday moment hinges on certain things. If the enemy can take our perspective, then he can alter our focus. Before we know it, we are in neverland somewhere trying to figure out how we got there. The truth has not changed, but our focus on it has. If the enemy can alter our focus, then he can steal our joy. Once we get focused on the temporal instead of the eternal, the slippery slope ensues. There is not much joy in the temporal. Paul said that he was outwardly (temporally) dying, but inwardly (eternally) being renewed day by day. Once we become conscious of sin or situations, our perspective changes our focus to self. Once the focus turns self-conscious, there is nothing you can do. We will lose our joy because everything focuses on the temporal. If the enemy can steal our joy, then he can steal our strength because the two are related. The Bible says that the joy of the Lord is my strength[2]. Once the enemy takes us down the road of lost perspective to misguided focus to robbed joy to stolen strength, the only thing that can help is a daybreak. Friend, your daybreak is on the way. As sure as tonight will turn into day, your night will turn into day. It is always darkest before the dawn of a new day. Get ready!! God's plan is coming. The resurrection is on the way. Our perspective is going to be restored. Our focus is going to be right. Our joy will be given back to us, and our strength will cease to wither. The resurrection is coming.

What guarantees a resurrection? Peter said in his sermon in Acts chapter 2 that it was **impossible** for death to hold him down. What made it impossible? In 1 Corinthians 15:20, the Bible declares that Christ rose from the dead, being the first fruits of all who had fallen asleep. We cannot understand this passage without a working knowledge of the Hebraic idea of first fruit. We have been taught our whole lives that first fruit and tithes were the same thing. In fact, they are not even related to each other. The first fruit was the part of the crop that came up first. If you planted a field, then there would be part of that field that would be ready for harvest first. The farmer had to harvest this part of the crop or it would ruin on the vine. The part of the crop that was considered first fruit (Hebrew word *bikkurim*) had to be sanctified for the whole crop to be sanctified. What is true of the first fruit is true of the whole crop. For first fruits (*bikkurim*) to be sanctified it had to become *terumah*. In order to become *terumah* (English translations: Heave offering, Wave Offering, Tribute, High offering, Most Holy Offering), the first fruit had to be lifted high and placed into the hands of the spiritual authority. When this happened, the whole crop was considered sanctified as unto the Lord. This caused the multiplication of wealth, increase, a blessing to rest on the house and revelation to fill the being[3]. The *terumah* offering became the key to everything they did. It was roughly one-fortieth of the income directly to the person's priest.

When Jesus was crucified, He would have had to become *terumah* or He would have been tainted. He was the first fruits which meant that He had to become *terumah*. In order for Jesus to become *terumah*, He had to be lifted high and placed into the hands of His spiritual authority. He was obviously lifted high on the cross. Jesus said, "Behold, if I be lifted high, I will draw all men to myself." Also, at the last moments of His life, He cried out, "Father, **into your hands** I commit my spirit." He is the *terumah* of God.

This process guaranteed the resurrection. Romans 11:16 declares, *"If the part of the dough offered as first fruits is holy, then the whole batch is holy; if the root is holy, so are the branches."* In other words, what is true of the first fruit is true of everything that is a part of it. This is exciting. In Isaiah, it says that He was a sacrifice for our transgressions and iniquities. What about His spirit? His spirit was placed into His Father's hands as a *terumah*. He was actually two offerings on the cross. This is why Peter could say that it was impossible for death to hold him. The first fruit of His spirit is in the hands of God. The whole lump now has to follow. To put this in story form, picture the following storyline. In order to guarantee the resurrection, Jesus places His spirit into the hands of His Father. He dies and experiences death, hell and the grave. Three days later, His father cries out from Heaven to give His Son back. When Satan asked for a basis, the Father said because the first fruits are in my hand. Now the whole lump has to follow; give Him back! Jesus giving His spirit as the first fruits offering guaranteed His resurrection because it guaranteed that the parts of Him that looked dead would come back to life due to the principle that the whole lump has to follow the first fruit.

The same is true in our life. When we get 'saved', we give our 'heart' to Jesus. Our heart is the root of who we are, so the heart acts as the first fruit. Therefore, our eternal life is guaranteed. It might look dead, but it is not. We are guaranteed eternal life. The same thing that guaranteed Jesus' resurrection now guarantees ours. When we place our heart in His hands, the lump has to follow. My body can die and waste away, but my spirit is being renewed day-by-day.

This is also true of other areas. If the first fruits of our finances are with God, then our finances can't die. They might look like they have been beaten to death, but they will resurrect. Any area in our life where the principle of first fruit is in place, there is no death because God has the first fruit. The whole lump has to follow.

Friend, if you have been living from Friday to Sunday, I want to tell you that Sunday is on the way. It is!! The King is standing on the beach waiting. He is waiting for our perspective to place Him in enough focus to restore our soul. That is what He longs to do. We have to keep our thoughts focused on the eternal things. God has got this in control. Once the perspective is right, the rest will follow, and we have taken a major step towards allowing the wellspring in our spirit out into the rest of the world.

Chapter Five

Endnotes
1. Psalm 30:5
2. Nehemiah 8:10
3. Proverbs 3:9,10; Nehemiah 10:35; Ezekiel 44:30; Matthew 6:22,23

6
DO I REALLY MATTER?

In the previous five chapters, we have discussed at length many facets of a withered soul. We have discussed what a withered soul looks like; how we get there; and what is the real truth surrounding our situations? At this point the book will take a turn and focus more on solutions. One of the most frustrating things about growing up in church is hearing a long list of utopian ideals from a stage where a man is separated from me by a huge pulpit while never understanding how to get to the utopia he is talking about.

Pick any sin issue, and I can tell you how most pastors address it from the pulpit. For example, let's say the topic for the day is lust. The pastor will proclaim in a loud voice the truth that lust is an abomination unto God. God hates it, and we should rid it from our lives. He will make three alliterated points: One, the reality of lust; Two, the result of lust; Three, the reward of lust. After 35 minutes of 'good preaching', the speaker leaves us with the incredible life changing advice of 'quit lusting'. WOW!! I do not know how he came up with that one. My life is changed. I now know that the problem of lust in my life needs to be stopped. The amazing part is that he screams it like I did not know that when I walked in the sanctuary that day. I just heard a 35 minute dissertation on the pain of lust and the pleasure of a life without lust, yet I have no idea how to transition my life to a place where I am lust-free. Have you ever experienced the same frustration? Have you ever screamed inside "Tell me how?"

This is also true of things that are not sin. For example, let's say the topic for the day is prayer. We get the same screaming, pulpit pounding and alliterated dissertation: One, pray with power; Two, pray with presence; Three, pray with persistence;

Four, pray with persuasion. Once again, we are left with the question of how. How do I pray with power? How do I pray "In Jesus' name?" How do I access it? How do I keep my mind from wandering during prayer? Very rarely do we answer the 'how to' questions. We leave church that day with the knowledge of what our prayer life would look like if it were perfect.

Probably the worst thing about both scenarios is the guilt that ensues. In situations like this, there is usually an 'altar call' at the end of the service to persuade people to make a commitment based on what they heard that day. People flock down to the altar to confess of lust in their life or their lack of prayer. They promise God that they will never lust again and will begin praying an hour a day starting tomorrow. However, they have been given no tools on how to fulfill any of those commitments. They simply have made a blind commitment in the face of horrible guilt. This is a recipe for disaster. The people have no chance of keeping their commitment which further reinforces the thought that they are failures. The withering of the soul perpetuates.

With this in mind, I want to dedicate the next few chapters to our responsibility in restoring the soul. God does all the work. Absolutely!! However, I need to understand how I position myself in the way of what He is doing. How do I become God-conscious instead of self-conscious? How do I overcome fear, guilt, anger, doubt, isolation and settling? How do I get out of the place of Lo Debar? How???

First of all, given the topics discussed in the first five chapters, we need to step back, take a deep breath, and remind ourselves of how much we really matter. My life is not by any means happenstance. My life is on purpose to the maximum degree. It is so full of purpose that God took time to write His dream down about me before time began. That is huge!! As if God does not have anything better to do than dream a purpose for my life. Consider the following scriptures:

> *For you created my inmost being; you knit me together in my mother's womb. I praise you because I am fearfully and wonderfully made; your works are wonderful, I know that full well. My frame was not hidden from you when I was made in the secret place. When I was woven together in the depths of the earth, your eyes saw my unformed body. All the days ordained for me were written in your book before one of them came to be. How precious to me are your thoughts, O God! How vast is the sum of them!*
>
> *-- Psalm 139:13-17*

> *One of them, an expert in the law, tested him with this question: "Teacher, which is the greatest commandment in the Law?" Jesus replied: "'Love the Lord your God with all your heart and with all your soul and with all your mind.' This is the first and greatest commandment. And the second is like it: 'Love your neighbor as yourself.' All the Law and the Prophets hang on these two commandments."*
>
> *-- Matthew 22:35-40*

Chapter Six

When Jesus was asked to sum up the key to the abundant life, He said the answer is to love God and love others **as you love yourself.** Surely, I am not the only person who knows someone who I would rather them **not** love me as they love themselves. They hate themselves!! It could be murder for them to love me as they love themselves. One of the ways that the church's message sets people up for failure is that it equates Biblical self-denial with non-Biblical self-abasement. For some reason, people have this idea that self-abasement is good, and self-esteem is bad. There is some merit to that thought if you skew the meanings of the words to the extreme. However, why not teach the truth and leave it at that. The fact that God carefully and purposefully constructed every single part of my being should leave me feeling important, confident and secure. It is not pride to feel those things when those things are based on what God did instead of what I did. It is not pride to have confidence in my calling when my calling is established before time began by the Supreme Person of the universe. It is not pride to feel important when the Bible clearly says that I am important enough for God to write a book about me. That is pretty important!!

Look at the scripture from Psalms. Is that not a confession of someone coming to grips with his worth to his Creator? Look at the intimacy in his imagery. He says God "knit him together in his mother's womb." In other words, we must realize that everything that gives us worth was put there before we had anything to do with it. There is no room for pride in that. We had nothing to do with it. God did it wonderfully. He did not knit us together half-way. We must come to the awareness that we are God's masterpiece; a wonderful work of art intricately put together by the master; a wonderful creation with each part placed in the right place to fulfill the right purpose; a creation which God took to a secret room with just He and us and spoke a dream into our hearts. In that private session, He whispered in our ear His incredible dream for our lives. He then stepped outside the room and wrote everything He said into a book that will define our destiny. Please get the picture.

Out of all the people in the world, He took you to a secret place, a romantic love nest where you and He can be intimate. The Groom whispers in your ear how much He believes in you. He tells you His dream for your life, and then takes the time to journal it in His special Book to be left by the bedside in order to remind you of that dream. Regularly, you might hear a gentle whisper from your Groom reminding you of that conversation that happened before time began. He is reminding you of His plan. You are His masterpiece. He thought of you, and made you completely unique. The Bible is clearly telling us that we are infinitely valuable to our Creator. Our mission is set in His book and if we do not position ourselves in it, then something in the cosmos is being left undone. That is how important we are.

How did we get messed up?

Anytime we begin to assess our worth and ponder the meaning of life, we ask three basic questions. The three basic questions of life are: Who am I; Why am I here; and Where am I going? People everywhere are in a pursuit of the answer to these questions, so they find them. There is no shortage of theories regarding the answer to these questions. When we begin to buy into the answers to these questions that are not found in the Bible, we start a process of withering where the root is found in the core of our existence. We are all wired to struggle with the basic questions of life. When we start finding our value by what we are made of (our matter, substance; how we look, our intelligence; emotional equilibrium, etc…) instead of the One who made us, it creates an incorrect assessment of self-worth. What are some of the influences?

Darwinism

This theory basically says that we all came together by chance, even on the cellular level. The cells in my body came together over years of trial and error by chance. One day, the moon and stars which came together by chance aligned just right, and I manifested. In other words, we are an accident. We just happened. There is no purpose, plan, or Book written by a Supreme God over my life. No divine pathway to shape our lives. We just happened. Think about the implications of that to our self-worth. Can you imagine being a child that was not planned and your parent telling you for the entirety of your life that you were an accident? You just happened!! There is no purpose because you were an accident. This theory gives us no basis for an abundant life because it strips us of our substance. Plus, it takes much more faith to believe this than it does to believe that the God of the universe carefully designed me with His purpose in mind. How much faith does it take to believe that all the parts of your eye just happened to fall together at the right place and time so that you can see? Even if you only had one eye, that would be highly unlikely, but most people have two eyes that work. What is the probability of all the rods, cones, retina, macula, iris, lens, pupil, optic nerve and cornea lining up perfectly by chance? It takes too much faith for me to believe that. This theory has influenced our culture in a major way, and it skews how we view ourselves away from a unique masterpiece to a happenstance 'cookie cutter'.

Existentialism

This theory says that we exist just to exist. Think about what that means for five minutes. It will blow the mind because it means nothing. Whatever will be will be? Our meaning comes from the process of simple existence. Nothing matters other than existence. The problem with this is that it leads us nowhere. There is no greater end than us. This only works when things are going superbly. When our existence is defined by happiness and success, this theory holds water. However, the minute the first person is unfulfilled, this theory starts sinking quickly. We have to be defined by something greater than mere existence because we all will die. This gives us no hope. The eminent nature of death necessarily means that we are worthless. This theory is destructive, and has influenced thought in a great way.

Futilism

This theory says that the answers to the first two questions are unknown. We cannot know where we came from, and we cannot know why we are here. We simply know where we are going, and that is death. Therefore, since our origins and our purpose are unknown, we can simply define our lives by how much fun we have. Live it up. Eat, drink, and be merry for tomorrow we die.

There are many problems with all of the above theories. However, the main issue is that all of them define a person as determined instead of unique. If we are determined, then the matter that makes us up is the only thing that determines our value. In other words, if we are intelligent, then we are more valuable than unintelligent people. If we are pretty, then we are more valuable than ugly people. The problem with being defined by our matter is that our matter is dying. Our outward man (matter) is being destroyed day by day because of sin[1]. I used to be able to grab the rim while playing basketball. I am lucky to get the net now because I have an extra thirty pounds strapped to my body. That is life. Athletes lose their athleticism; sharp people dull; homecoming queens wrinkle and expand; homecoming kings become couch potatoes. When our worth is found in our matter, we are signing up to lose. Our worth cannot be found in our looks, intelligence, earning potential, job, wealth or titles. Our worth has to be found in the substance of our spirit.

Our worth has to be about something bigger than us. That is the conclusion David comes to in Psalm 139. If my worth is not found in what my Creator thinks of me, then everything I do loses value. Notice the scripture from Ecclesiastes 1:14,

> *"I have seen all the things that are done under the sun; all of them are meaningless, a chasing after the wind."*

Once we get in this rut, several things happen. Firstly, our vitality leaves. The things that used to matter to us begin not to matter. We start to lose our passion for the things that we would have died for at one time. We just cannot seem to find the energy. If it does not matter, then why should we care?

Secondly, our relationships suffer. The reason is that our self-worth becomes a filter for how we relate to people. When our self-worth is based on determined matter, no one can meet our expectations. We cannot be pleased because we are number one. This makes community and relationships that God honors impossible. Thirdly, our potential declines. The longer we look at things other than God to define our self-worth, the more often we will come to conclusion that we really do not matter. Outside of God, we do not matter for it is in Him we live and move and **have our being**[2]. In other words, our existence is meaningless outside of His plan that He whispered in my heart before time began. It is meaningless outside of what is written in His love journal to me.

Action Points

One major difference between Hebraic thought and Greek thought is that Greek people think thoughts and Hebraic people feel thoughts. Westernized culture comes from Greek thinking. We learn to think in bullet points. We seldom feel anything because we are taught to ignore our feelings and 'live by faith'. Crazy! However, that is what we are taught. For example, a Greek minded person will read that Christ has forgiven all our sins, and will think about it and move on. On the other hand, a Hebrew minded person will stop and feel the truth that they are totally and completely innocent in His sight. What a difference! In Bible college, I wrote many papers on the theology of God, yet I never felt the truth of what I was writing. I believed it, but did not feel it. When is the last time you felt the truth that all of Christ lives in you? When is the last time you felt the truth that you are completely innocent? When is the last time you felt the truth that perfect peace lives in you?

Chapter Six

We have to internalize the truths expressed in this chapter. I want you to have some thoughts that are rooted so deep inside that you feel the truth of them. Think about this fifteen times a day for the next month: "My life is made on purpose." Think it until you feel it. The Bible calls it meditation — to think about a thought until you feel the truth of it. Think about the fact that a purpose was given to you by almighty God. Think about it until you sense the emotion tied to the excitement of the truth that there is something out there God designed you for that only you can do. Internalize the confidence of knowing you are the person for the job. No one can do it like you. No one! God wrote down this purpose and it is set. Feel the confidence. Feel the importance. Feel the job security in knowing that you are the only one who can do what He called you to do.

The next thought we need to meditate on is this: "I am molded after the image of my Creator." Think about that fifteen times a day. Experience the worth in that. We are made in the image of God. We are molded after the perfection of our Creator. God carefully fashioned us to look like Him. Feel that. Internalize the fact that He thought enough of us to make us in His image. Sense the acceptance in that. There is no rejection in that. It is pure, uncensored acceptance. Feel it as often as you can.

The last thought we need to meditate on is this: "God looked at me and is specifically pleased with me." Our Groom can't wait to be intimate with us. He loves us and is pleased with us. He knows that we are perfectly made to carry out His dream for our lives. Sense His pleasure coming around you. Feel it twenty times a day. We do not have to try to feel unworthy for that is a natural emotion. We have to train ourselves to internalize the truth that He is pleased with us which makes us worthy. We are not worthy because of our matter, behavior, intelligence, works, looks, etc... We are worthy because He is pleased with us. When is the last time you felt His pleasure on you? Feel it now. It is true! He died for you to have the right to feel His pleasure. Now think about it. Meditate on it day and night until that feeling replaces the old feeling of unworthiness.

Do I really matter? Yes, you matter! You are completely unique and God's plan for you is written. Your worth is as infinite as the most priceless metals, jewels and precious stones because He owns it all and still made you unique. Your Creator is waiting in the secret place ready to breathe over you a word that will propel you to your destiny. He wrote His dream in a Book. Read that Book!!! Think that Book!!! Feel the feelings your Groom has over you. You are the most important person in the whole world to Him.

Endnotes
1. Colossians 3:10
2. Acts 17:28

SHAME "OFF" YOU

7

WITH A NAME LIKE SHANE, I have heard no shortage of puns pertaining to the word shame. I have a family member that used to sing the song "Shame on you, for hurting me" in my general direction all the time. She would conveniently change the word shame for my name. I think she really thought it was funny as evidenced by the fact that she laughed hysterically every time she did it for over ten years.

I met a man once with a completely mangled arm. I asked him what happened to him, and he told me that his parents had purposely broken his arm in that way in order to make him a better beggar. He grew up in the beggar class of the caste system in India. In that culture, the caste that you are born into determines worth. As a beggar, his arm was meaningless unless it made him a better beggar, so his authority made him the best beggar he could be by deforming his arm. This man's story broke my heart. His sense of his being was affected by the caste system he was born into. The shame of the class was projected onto his life.

Learning to align ourselves in the way of God's heart to restore our soul is our responsibility. Part of that responsibility comes with understanding the difference between shame and guilt. Feelings of shame are bad feelings about ourselves because of who we are. Feelings of guilt are bad feelings about ourselves because of what we have done. Shame has to do with the core of our identity. It deals with who we are. It deals with the substance of our being. When we feel ashamed, it has to do with the definition of ourselves.

In an earlier chapter, we discussed the life of Saul's grandson, Mephibosheth. He was the son of the king, yet he described himself as a 'dead dog'[1]. Based on who he was, the son of a former king, he felt that the new king would treat him like a 'dead dog'. That was the tradition of the day. He had no rights. However, the king allowed him to dine at his table and retain all of his land. Basically, David told him that he had nothing to be ashamed of because he was in covenant with his king.

People deal with guilt on a daily basis because of things they have done. They have failed for the first time in a certain area of sin, or they have failed for the hundredth time in the same area of sin. Regardless, the feelings of guilt begin to take over. A person might fight sin a hundred times in a day and win ninety-eight of those battles, yet the two defeats win the awareness battle and the person goes to bed feeling completely defeated. This is a critical point in the soul's withering process. Does the person connect the guilt from the sin with the shame of being a sinner?

Sometimes a person makes the mistake of convincing themselves that the Holy Spirit is convicting them of being a sinner. That is not a function of the Holy Spirit. Notice what Jesus says about the role of the Holy Spirit in John 16:8-11:

> *"When he comes, he will convict the world of guilt in regard to sin and righteousness and judgment: in regard to sin, because men do not believe in me; in regard to righteousness, because I am going to the Father, where you can see me no longer; and in regard to judgment, because the prince of this world now stands condemned."*

The Holy Spirit's role in conviction is three-fold. The word for conviction in this passage is *elegcho* which contains the idea of convincing. First of all, the passage says that the Holy Spirit is going to convince the world of sin **because men do not believe in me.** In other words, the Holy Spirit's job is to convince the unbeliever that he is a sinner and needs to believe. This is the conviction that leads to repentance for salvation.

Secondly, the passage indicates that He will convince people of righteousness. Who are the righteous ones? The people who believe in Jesus for the forgiveness of sins have been recreated in righteousness and true holiness[2]. Their sins do not count against them[3], nor does God remember their sin[4]. The Holy Spirit convinces a saved person that they are the righteousness of God in Christ. He does not convince a saved person of guilt for sin because He does not even remember their sin nor count their sin against them. Consider the following scripture:

> *Therefore, if anyone is in Christ, he is a new creation; the old has gone, the new has come! All this is from God, who reconciled us to himself through Christ and gave us the ministry of reconciliation: that God was reconciling the world to himself in Christ,* ***not counting men's sins against them****. And he has committed to us the message of reconciliation.*
>
> *--2 Corinthians 5:17-19*

Let's ask ourselves an honest question. If God does not remember our sin nor count it against us because of the blood of His Son, then how is He in the business of convincing us that we are sinners? The answer is that He is not in that business. He loves to convince a person that he is righteous. When the conviction of righteousness gets deep enough into a person, then the behavior and acts of righteousness take care of themselves. Many readers at this point need to stop and think about their innocence before God. In God's eyes, there is not one sin on our record. NOT ONE!! They have been erased, blotted out, thrown as far as the east is from the west[5]. They are gone, gone, gone. As you stand before the presence of God, He will not bring up one thing that you did wrong because He does not remember!! You are completely accepted by God.

Thirdly, He is convincing the prince of this world that he stands condemned. What an awesome picture this paints. The Holy Spirit is convincing sinners that there is hope in Christ. He is convincing Christ-followers that their hope is secure because they have been recreated in righteousness and true holiness, and He is convincing the enemy that he is defeated. The next time the enemy seems to be beating down our doorstep, we can take heart to know that the Holy Spirit is on his doorstep reminding him of his future. He has no hope. He is a completely defeated foe.

With the above truths in mind, it is so important that we never let the acts of a guilty conscious convince us that we are not righteous. This creates a works mentality with God that spirals us downward. Romans 3:20 says that "No one will be declared righteous in his sight by observing the law; rather, through the law we become conscious of sin." We are declared righteous by grace through faith[6]. When guilt turns to shame, we cheapen grace. We despise the Spirit of grace. The Holy Spirit is gently trying to convince us that we are righteous and we cheapen

His effort by putting so much credence in our own work. The problem is that we vastly overestimate our own righteousness and greatly underestimate what He did on the cross. We tend to take ourselves way too seriously! The point is that a person is not defined by what he does. Rather, he is defined by who he is. There is no room for shame in Christ because shame deals with the core of who we are. Our substance is absolutely perfect without one blemish whatsoever. For any person in Christ to be ashamed, they have dangerously confused the role of shame and guilt.

What are some symptoms of confusing our identity? How do I know if I need shame to be removed off of me? Here are a few symptoms. Firstly, a person can become hypercritical. When a person feels like a failure, they tend to project that feeling onto anything and anybody. They begin to nit-pick everything. They feel like a failure, so their existence gets pleasure from making other people feel like a failure. It is therapeutic. Typically, people who are the most critical and sin-conscious are the people who feel the worst about themselves. They are the people with the lowest sense of security with God. The anxiety that comes from that state forces people to make other people feel the same way. Secondly, a person can change who they are just to fit in. The person full of shame wants to feel accepted so badly that they will become anything just to feel the acceptance. Thirdly, a person full of shame will find themselves boasting. When the insecurity hits a new height, the person feels as though they have to tell people all their good so that no one will notice the many places in which they do not measure up. This is a dangerous relational rut that only further shows our problem with shame and guilt.

Action Points

We have to back up and do a true self-assessment. Where are we in terms of our belief system concerning our standing with God? Do I really believe with all my heart that I am innocent in His sight? When is the last time I felt that truth? Do I really believe that He does not remember my sin? Do I really believe that He does not count my sin against me? Do I project my unbelief onto others only to make them more sin-conscious? Friends, these are all truths straight from the Bible. If they disagree with how we have been taught, then we need to change our thinking. We do not need to make the Bible fit what our mom, dad or church denomination thinks. Changing our thinking in this key area is a must for the restoration of our soul. Our soul is a feeling entity. If the soul cannot feel the restoration, then it is really not restoration. God has laid this amazing plan before us. All the sin is gone! All the shame is gone! You are guilt-free before the Creator of the universe! We have to believe that. Really believe that!

Secondly, we need to consider what God has already done to move toward us. Anytime a created being is questioning its worth, the best place for it to go is its Creator. What does my Creator think of me? What are His thoughts? What lengths has He gone to show me how He feels? We need to think deeply about these truths. Firstly, God took all the initiative to make a plan to reconnect with you. He made the first call. He made the action plan. We had nothing to do with it. All the way back at Genesis 3:15 and throughout the entire Bible, we read of God's relentless pursuit of mankind. He wants to reconcile the world to Himself, and has made all the provision to do so. God moved first. That is an extreme act of love demonstrated to us with no merit of our own. That is how much He thinks of us. He moved first even though it would cost Him everything. He could have destroyed His creation, moved on, and started over. However, He thought enough of each of us to make the first move towards reconciliation. Is that not the toughest move? Think about the last relational trial you had. The toughest move is the first one because it holds the biggest risk of rejection. Our Creator was willing to take all the risk. He loves us with an everlasting love that is unquenchable. Think about that deeply until you can sense the truth of it. God made the first move toward you.

Thirdly, He gave His Son for you. John 3:16 says that "God loved the world so much that He gave His only Son that whoever believes in Him will never die but have eternal life." This begins to show the depth of His love. Doubtless, many people reading this book are parents. Being parents, you know of people who you would die for, namely, your own children. However, you probably cannot think of one person who you would let your own child die for. That is the depth of love that our Creator has for us. It is deeper than His willingness to die for us. It is that He loved us so much that He gave His only Son to die for us. How does that make you feel? Your Creator, the One who determines your worth, is willing to give His only Son for you. There is no room for shame in that. Friend, you are so precious in His sight that He was willing to move Heaven to Earth just for you. He was willing to watch His Son die just for you. That should begin to remove any sense of shame because it removes any doubt of our worth.

Fourthly, He died for you with no guarantee of you choosing Him. Romans 5:8 says that "God commends His love for us in that while we were sinners Christ died for the ungodly." He died for us with no guarantee. He died for us while we were in our most unworthy state. He gave us the greatest act of love while we were still ungodly. Why do we still insist that He is impressed with our righteousness now? No, our righteousness is as filthy rags[7]. He is not impressed with us. He is impressed with Christ. The greatest act of love was given because of grace while we were still sinners, and the acts of love from here on out will be because of grace as well. God reached down in our state of disgrace and replaced it with grace. Grace does not mean as much without disgrace. Our Creator took us from a disgraced work of art on the shelf to a spectacular masterpiece recreated without one blemish. What a thought!! Think that thought twenty times today, and the shame will begin to lose its power.

Fifthly, He is building you a house. John 14 says that He is going to prepare a place for us that where He is there we can be also. This is ancient Hebraic wedding language. The Bible is including some intimate language here to show us how our Creator feels about us. When a bride and groom to be would complete the engagement process, they would stand and the groom would say the above statement as quoted in John 14. He is speaking about the wedding chamber that his father has to approve before the marriage can be consummated. Understand His point! Our Creator is making a special marriage chamber for just us and Him. He is decorating it just like we would want it, and He is longing to be completely one with us. He is building you a perfect place. He loves you so much that He is designing every intricate detail of your eternal dwelling.

Sixthly, He desires to be with you forever. Many of us have great friends that we love to be with. However, for most of those friends, there comes that time of night where it is time for them to go home. We love them, but we have had our fill. Only the truest loves of our lives do we want to be with as much as possible. God looks at you that way. He wants to be with you for all eternity. That is love!! He wants to be with you forever, and ever and ever. That puts His love in perspective.

Friend, we need to put how our Creator feels about us in the forefront of our minds. He determines our worth because He made us. There is no shame. NONE! Guilt has been taken care of on the cross. He has done everything possible to declare His love for us. We simply have to walk into His love and receive it. We have to think about the truths in this chapter until those feelings override our guilt and shame. Our Creator is screaming at His masterpiece that He loves us. He made us perfect. He made us with no blemish. Hear Him!!! He is screaming "SHAME 'OFF' YOU!"

Endnotes
1. 2 Samuel 9:8
2. Ephesians 4:24
3. 2 Corinthians 5:20
4. Hebrews 8
5. Psalm 103:12
6. Romans 3:21-24
7. Isaiah 64:6

8
Embracing Your Acceptance with God

Lying in my bed that night at twelve years old was no piece of cake. I could not fall asleep, and my mind was tormented. I tossed and turned for hours. I spent time yearning for God to hear the cry of my heart as to how much I loved Him. I cried for the longest time partially because I was upset and partially because I thought God would think I was serious if I was crying. I would get up periodically just to make sure my parents were still in bed. I was terrified. What happened to me to get me this upset? I heard a sermon!

That's right. I heard a passionate, pulpit-pounding message from God's Word that left me terrified. Have you ever heard a preacher that was so good at painting a picture that you could feel every word he was saying? A good communicator can do that. It works well for the listener until the preacher can take the person into the very inner room of hell itself. The preacher that day went through this incredible story of a chemical burn victim whose burn would ignite when contacted with water because of the chemical residue on the skin. Imagine where that message went.

He painted a vivid picture of a man screaming in agony from the burn only to be placed in more agony when the physicians ignorantly put him in water. He closed his message by proclaiming, "That is exactly what will happen to you if you die in your sin or if Jesus comes back before you repent." Whoa! I felt every crevice of hell and became so frightened that Jesus would forget me if He came back. I started thinking of every sin that I had ever even thought about. Someone might be asking, "What's wrong with a sermon like that?" The answer is nothing. Sermons like that are very effective at convincing people without Christ that they need Him. However, I was a believer in Christ. I had come to a place in my life where that I knew that I could not save myself and placed my life completely in the hands of Christ. I knew that my only hope for forgiveness and holiness was found in Christ. However, this sermon succeeded in making me so sin-conscious that I doubted my standing with God.

I crossed a line that day. I moved from faith in Jesus for the forgiveness of my sins to faith in myself being able to 'get it right'. I could not have explained it that way at that point because even in the sixth grade I had memorized Ephesians 2:8,9—

> *"For by grace you have been saved through faith, and not of yourself, it is the gift of God not of works, so that no man can boast."*

Every evangelical Christian believes that. However, I wonder how many of us have ever doubted our salvation because of something we have done? We believe in salvation by grace through faith, yet we doubt the grace when there is sin-consciousness. Paul said that where sin abounds grace abounds much more[1]. He also warned of the implications of defining our life by getting it right. Romans 3:20 says,

> *"Therefore, no one will be declared righteous in his sight by observing the law; rather, through the law we become conscious of sin."*

In other words, to try to maintain a relationship with God by getting it all right will only make someone aware of where they get it wrong. I was only in the sixth grade, yet I was already learning the principle that sin-consciousness leads me nowhere.

I was so aware of where I missed it with God that I was convinced that His grace was not sufficient for me.

When we define our lives this way, it necessarily withers our soul because it connects our thoughts, feelings and will to our own effort and behavior. Eventually, we will be let down. Eve made this mistake in the garden. She traded perfect oneness with God for a chance to be like God. The serpent told her that if she ate of the tree of knowledge of good and evil that she would be like God[2]. Why would she want to be like God when she had perfect oneness with God? Why would she ever trade oneness for likeness? Why do we trade the truth of 'Christ in us' for a chance to be 'like Christ'? What a rip off! We trade oneness with Christ for a chance to define our life by how well we master good and evil so that we can be like Christ. That is a bad deal, yet people make that trade all the time. We allow ourselves to own oneness with Christ, yet we feel our own insecurity, sinfulness, guilt, shame, and imperfection based on our ability to master 'good and evil'. Please hear me! This is a bad deal. This leads us to a place of bondage and self-consciousness that vastly limits our potential.

The Apostle Paul was screaming about this very principle throughout his writings especially in Galatians 3 and Colossians 2. I would encourage the readers to take time and specifically study these two awesome passages of scripture. Please allow me to summarize the content of those passages in the following few sentences. With their own effort, a person cannot complete what was initiated with God's grace. If it started with grace, then it finishes with grace. The key to living as one with Christ is to continue with the same principle, which is faith in Him that provided our salvation. A person's spirituality is never found in what he does or does not handle, taste or touch. His spirituality is found in his faith, and in that faith is a perfect oneness with Christ where God is bound by covenant to complete the good work He started in the person. Consider the following excerpts from the stated scripture:

> *"So then, just as you received Christ Jesus as Lord, continue to live in him,"*
>
> *--Colossians 2:6*
>
> *"Since you died with Christ to the basic principles of this world, why, as though you still belonged to it, do you submit to its rules: "Do not handle! Do not taste! Do not touch!"? These are all destined to perish with use, because they are based on human commands and teachings."*
>
> *-- Colossians 2:20-22*
>
> *"Are you so foolish? After beginning with the Spirit, are you now trying to attain your goal by human effort?"*
>
> *--Galatians 3:3*
>
> *"But the Scripture declares that the whole world is a prisoner of sin, so that what was promised, being given through faith in Jesus Christ, might be given to those who believe. Before this faith*

> *came, we were held prisoners by the law, locked up until faith should be revealed. So the law was put in charge to lead us to Christ that we might be justified by faith. Now that faith has come, we are no longer under the supervision of the law. You are all sons of God through faith in Christ Jesus, for all of you who were baptized into Christ have clothed yourselves with Christ."*

--Galatians 3:22-27

The point is simply that if we are saved by grace, then we keep it by grace. If the favor of God is by grace, then it stays on us by grace. We cannot earn acceptance from God. God is giving it away. We just have to live in that acceptance. When we live in that acceptance, then our behavior will take care of itself because we would never want to trample the grace that was given to us.

What principles did God set in place in order to guarantee our position with Him? There is a three-fold interlocking act of God that guarantees our place with Him in intimacy. The three acts are found in Romans 3:20-26:

> *"Therefore no one will be declared righteous in his sight by observing the law; rather, through the law we become conscious of sin. But now a righteousness from God, apart from law, has been made known, to which the Law and the Prophets testify. This righteousness from God comes through faith in Jesus Christ to all who believe. There is*

> *no difference, for all have sinned and fall short of the glory of God, and are **justified** freely by his grace through the **redemption** that came by Christ Jesus. God presented him as a **sacrifice of atonement**, through faith in his blood. He did this to demonstrate his justice, because in his forbearance he had left the sins committed beforehand unpunished-- he did it to demonstrate his justice at the present time, so as to be just and the one who justifies those who have faith in Jesus."*

The teaching of this passage of scripture should set people free. There is a declaration of righteousness that is apart from how well we keep the rules. The passage starts by saying that no one will be declared right with God by keeping all the rules. However, there is righteousness from God that is based on three interlocking acts. This is apart from the law and is available for all sinners.

The first act is justification. The word for justification in the Greek language is *dikaioo*. This is a very common word used in that time in the courts of the day. It was a legal term. It would have been used in accordance with a gavel by a judge to declare people not guilty. The judge would lower the gavel and declare *dikaioo*. Not guilty, not guilty, not guilty. We need to take time and build that sense into our lives. We are innocent in His sight because we have been declared not guilty in His court. No charge can stand against us because Jesus Christ is our advocate, our lawyer. He is testifying on our behalf to have us declared not guilty. The Creator of the universe is guaranteeing our innocence based on His own Word that does not change. The

Bible says that we are now recreated in righteousness and true holiness. This is justification. We are made just as if we have never sinned one time. There is no sin on our record. Not one! It does us no good to scrutinize every act of the sinful nature until we doubt this. The grace of God has removed our sin as far as the east is from the west. We need to get that into us. We are completely and totally innocent.

The second act is redemption. The Greek word for redemption is *apolutrosis*. This word is a market place term. It would have been specifically used in the slave markets of the day to denote someone whose price had been paid to buy them out of slavery. In other words, our debt has been paid. We do not owe God anymore. He paid the price for our sin so that there would be no debt on our accounts. Can you picture it? You are standing on an auctioning block and all sorts of things are bidding for your life. Bitterness is bidding for your life. Anger is bidding for your life. Lust is bidding for your life. Pride, malice, slander, rage, gossip, disappointment and hate are bidding for your life. However, no matter how high the bidding gets, you have an Advocate in the crowd bidding against them. He is screaming at the top of His lungs, "YOU CANNOT HAVE HIM!!!" "HE IS MINE!!" He keeps outbidding them until it costs Him everything just to buy us. That is redemption. He redeemed us from the curse of the law[3]. What does that mean? Does it mean the law is null and void? NO!! It means that the price for breaking the law has been paid. We owe no debt on our account.

The third act is that Jesus is the sacrifice of atonement. This is just one word in the Greek language, *hilasterion*. Sometimes it is translated propitiation — to appease and satisfy wrath. This word is the same word used to translate the Hebrew word for *mercy seat*. The mercy seat was the place in the Holy of Holies where the priest would sprinkle the blood of the sacrifice. The mercy seat was located between the presence of God and the contents of the Ark of the Covenant. Inside the Ark was the law of God. In other words, the blood came between the presence of God and the standard of God. Therefore, when God looks at His standard, He now sees His standard through the blood. It is not that the standard has changed. Rather, the standard has been satisfied by the blood. There is no room for wrath for an unmet standard.

All three acts are necessary for intimacy to happen. If a person has justification and redemption without propitiation, then that person gets to spend eternity with an angry God. If a person has redemption and propitiation without justification, then he gets hell because he is sinful in God's sight. If a person has justification and propitiation without redemption, then he still owes God. In any case, we still come to the table of God with some debt. We still owe Him. Therefore, we come to His table with our own righteousness, and all we accomplish is throwing our filthy rags all over His nice table. He is sitting at His table wanting to dine with us, and we are trying to impress Him with our righteousness. How embarrassing!

Please hear the message of the Gospel. A person cannot impress God with his own righteousness. God is not impressed with filthy rags. He is impressed with Christ. He cannot notice our righteousness without noticing our unrighteousness because they are the flip side of the same works coin. Therefore, He gives us grace by choosing not to notice either one. He simply sees Christ.

Friend, you have been given oneness with Christ. Do not trade it for likeness!! Do not trade it for an opportunity to define your life by how well you master good and evil. Every person reading this book who is in Christ has been given perfect righteousness and holiness. We cannot be more holy than the holiness He gave us. He gave us His holiness. What can we do to improve on that? For our soul to connect to Him, we have to trust Him. Truly trust Him. He has given us acceptance with God. We just have to take it. Good and evil will never define you again. You are defined by His blood. He sees you through it. Now see yourself through it. You are completely accepted by Him by grace through faith. Step into that and allow the guilt, shame, insecurity and self-consciousness to fade away in the divine replacement of righteousness, holiness and pure acceptance. Proclaim loudly that He is restoring your soul.

Endnotes
1. Romans 5:20
2. Genesis 3:5
3. Galatians 3:13

Rebuilding Who You Really Are

9

THE YOUNG MAN sat in my office completely confused. He had messed up in the same area for what seemed like the millionth time. I really felt for him. He was so discombobulated and felt so condemned. Towards the end of this appointment, he made an interesting statement about the real person inside of him. He asked me how long it would take to rebuild who he really is to the point that he could live out of it. What a great question! Who am I? How can that person be rebuilt? How long will it take? I want to bring this book on restoring the soul to a close by giving some final action points on rebuilding the awareness of who we really are. A person can lose anything in the natural, and it will be rebuilt as long as they have the blueprint on the inside to rebuild it. We have to let our thoughts focus on who we really are as found in our spirit. We have to rebuild our spirit being.

God is working a process

The first action point to focus on is that God is working a process. He is in no hurry with any person. He never has been. Think about how God works. He promises Abraham that he would be the father of a great nation. Okay! We need a lot of things for that to happen: babies, land, law, leader, legacy, culture and a system to care for all the babies. The problem is that Abraham is already one hundred years old. God had His work cut out for Him. An entire generation went by and there was still only one person, Isaac. Another generation went by and there was still only one person, Jacob. We are three generations through this promise, and no sign of the fulfillment. We still have no babies, land, law, leader, legacy, culture or system. Did Abraham miss God? Did he uproot his success in Ur and walk 2000 miles with family, servants, camels, and livestock for nothing? It took four generations for there to be any evidence of the multiplication of people because Jacob had twelve children. However, there is still no land, law, leader, culture, legacy or system. Through a series of complicated events, the twelve end up in the land of Goshen which is owned by Egypt. Their descendants spent over four hundred years in Egypt before God provides a leader to take them out of slavery. After this, they wander the wilderness for forty years before the conquest of the land begins. After a long process of conquering the land, it finally looks as if the promise of a nation is coming to be. Finally, there are people, land, law, leader, culture and a system. The Torah had been established. This took approximately 580 years from promise to fulfillment. God is not in a hurry. To top it all off, the nation only existed for a few hundred years before it was divided and then eventually taken into captivity by Assyria and Babylon. This nation did not reestablish as an official nation until 1948.

God is not in a hurry. He is patient with His promise for our life. This is His pattern throughout scripture. Hebrews 11:32 says that Barak, Jephthah, Gideon, and Samson were all people of great faith. Look at their lives. Was God kidding? Jephthah sacrificed his own daughter on an altar he made. Samson lost it all for lust and approval. Gideon was the lowest person in his family. Barak was used greatly by God, but did not have the faith to go without Deborah. These men were heroes of the faith? God is not in a hurry. He is working a process. He is processing Simons to Peters; Jacobs to Israels; Sons of Thunder to Sons of Righteousness; and Sauls to Pauls. He is still in this business, and He is patient. He always sees the end from the beginning. Therefore, He sees you now for how you will be instead of how you are. His purposes will be fulfilled in our lives. When He starts something, then He is duty-bound to finish it according to Philippians 1:6. You are no exception. He began the good work in you, and He will complete it.

Let the past die

In Joshua 1 there is a paradigm shift in leadership from Moses to Joshua. Joshua is understandably overwhelmed with the new-found responsibility as well as the weight of grieving the death of his mentor. Out of all the grief, this loving voice from God comes to Joshua and says, "Moses my servant is dead, now arise." God skips all the empathy of the situation and tells him to render the past dead. He is the man now. This is his show to run. There is mission, vision and confidence in God's statement.

We oftentimes can find ourselves in similar situations. The pressure is now on us to handle a situation of epic proportions. We find ourselves asking many 'what if' questions. What if this would have gone differently? What if that would not have happened? What if…? What if…? What if…? Fill in the blanks. God is saying that for us to move forward and take hold of our destiny, we have to move out of the past and into our future with full force. Joshua would have never been who he could be while holding onto Moses' legacy. We have to move out of yesterday and into tomorrow. Think about that truth. Let the sense that today is a new day settle over you deeply. There is a line in the sand. It will never be the same from this day forward. Move into this new day with no strings attached to the past. This will move us into a position to be in the way of what God is doing.

Position yourself in organic environments

Plants do not have to try to grow in a greenhouse because the environment is right for growth. When the environment is right, then right things happen without us even trying. We need to practice placing ourselves in organic environments. One of the best suggestions a person could ever listen to when it comes to restoring the soul is to get into a community of people who breathe life into them. When we have a group that we do life together with where the environment is just right for growth, we cannot help but be restored.

On the other hand, we can choose to expose ourselves to toxic environments. If I took a plant and put it in a closet with no sunlight or water, then the plant would die without me trying to kill it. Unfortunately, some people run to toxic environments when they feel like their soul is sagging. This breathes death instead of life. The toxic environment contaminates our soul with doubt, fear, guilt, anger and isolation. It reinforces those things.

God is on a completely different page. He is working a process to restore our soul. We just have to cultivate soul health by choosing organic environments instead of toxic environments. When our soul is withered, we need a Christ-based community to interact with on a regular basis. We do not need people who remind us of our past, reinforce unhealthy behavior or are negative about our future. NO! We need a Christ-based community who always remind us of who we are instead of who we are not. They always remind us that God is giving us a hope and a future. Get into a small group like that.

Just as, so walk

Colossians 2:6,7 sums up living the Christian life in the most simplistic statement in the whole Bible. It states,

> "So then, **just as** you received Christ Jesus as Lord, **so walk** in Him."

That is the most simplistic explanation of walking with Christ. How do I walk with God? The answer is just like I received Him. We have made it so much harder than that. We have created formulas and patterns to walk with God that put people in jail to the basic principles that Paul said we died to. I have been told a plethora of things about walking with God - some of which border on the edge of insanity. For example, a very well-meaning person told me when I was a kid that God would know I was serious when I prayed if I would cry. Well, one can imagine what I did. I forced myself to cry when I prayed because I thought that God would honor it more. I have been told all sorts of things. I have been told to pray standing, pray bowing, pray kneeling, pray prostrate, pray with tears, pray with joy, pray with moaning, pray while screaming, pray with quiet fervor and to pray with 'holy' groaning. Please do not misunderstand me. I am not making fun. Everyone who told me these things meant well and thought it would help. They were only telling me what they had been taught.

The problem with this is that everyone was making it harder than 'just as, so walk'. I began to ask myself a good question. How did I receive Christ? The answer to that question holds the key to walking with God because it holds the first part to the equation of 'just as, so walk'. I began to reflect on my salvation experience that took place in the back of a sixth grade classroom. I put my trust in Christ for the forgiveness of sin and took His righteousness on instead of trying to create my own righteousness and holiness. I responded to the persuasion in my heart to make Christ the Lord of my life. I received the grace He was offering me and by faith entered into it. I opened my heart to His touch and received what He had for me, and I confessed with my mouth that God raised Him from the dead, and He was Lord of my life.

Let me make one observation about confession at this point. The word for confession is the Greek word *homologio* which comes from two words *homo* (the same) and *logos* (word). The correct definition of confession is to say the same word as or to agree with. Therefore, confessing our sin is simply agreeing with God that we are sinful. Think about the passage from 1 John 1:8,9. It says,

> *"If we say we are without sin, we deceive ourselves and the truth is not in us. If we confess (agree with) our sin, he is faithful and just to forgive us our sin and cleanse us from all unrighteousness."*

The Greek word for sin there is *hamartia* which has to do with general sin. It literally means anything we do that misses the center of the mark. Therefore, what 1 John is communicating is that if we believe we can create our own righteousness and never miss the center of the mark then we are deceived. However, if we will agree with the fact that we are sinful, then He will respond to that agreement with a just act to cleanse us from all unrighteousness.

In summary, I trusted, responded, received grace, opened my life and agreed with God. That is how I received Christ. If our lives with Him ever get more complicated than to continue trusting, responding, receiving grace when we miss it, and to continue agreeing with Him that He is the only way, then our lives are getting religious. We run the risk of crossing a line into faith in my good behavior to save me instead of faith in His righteousness. 'Just as, so walk' is the key to everything in the Christian life. Do you want to utilize your spiritual gifts? All you have to do is to trust, respond, receive and confess. Do you want to tap into the favor of God? Keep trusting, responding, receiving and confessing. Do you want to pray for someone for healing? Keep trusting, responding, receiving and confessing. We do not have to earn any special 'anointing'. We simply have to continue in how we entered into our relationship with Christ in the first place.

Living in Christ is not spelled DO it is spelled DONE.

I was reared in what I would consider a good home. God was the center of my life for as long as I can remember. However, I stayed confused about what God thought about me. I went to church at a Pentecostal Holiness church, yet I was educated at an independent Baptist school. There are not more direct opposite groups within the realm of Christianity. Jews and Muslims have more differences, but that is about it. My church and school only agreed on two things: Firstly, how to get saved and secondly, everything you could possibly think about doing is a sin. At church, if you sinned, God left. At school, if you sinned, God is mad. Which one is worse, going to hell or spending eternity with a really mad God? Both were full of

Chapter Nine

great people who helped form who I am, and I am deeply thankful to them. However, I was confused. It put a performance mentality in me so deeply that I thought God loved me when I did well, and hated me when I did wrong. This works well as long as everything is going great because if things are going great, then God loves me. If God loves me, then my life is right. However, if things go wrong, then God must be mad. If God is mad, then I must be doing something wrong. This idea will wreak havoc on our lives. At best case, we are in bondage to sin-consciousness.

I love the truth that Christ lived the life for me so that I can live out of Him. He is my life. Galatians 3 depicts this so beautifully that I want you to see it from the message translation:

> *"How did your new life begin? Was it by working your heads off to please God? Or was it by responding to God's Message to you? Are you going to continue this craziness? For only crazy people would think they could complete by their own efforts what was begun by God. If you weren't smart enough or strong enough to begin it, how do you suppose you could perfect it? "Does God do these things [good things in your life] because of your strenuous moral striving or because you trust him to do them in you?...The obvious impossibility of carrying out such a moral program should make it plain that no one can sustain a relationship with God that way...<u>Doing things for God is the opposite of entering into what God does for you.</u> Habakkuk (2:4) had it right: 'The person who*

> *believes God is set right by God—and that's the real life.' Rule keeping does not naturally evolve into living by faith, but only perpetuates itself in more rule keeping...Christ redeemed us from that self-defeating, cursed life by absorbing it completely into Himself...Therefore, we are all able to receive God's life, His Spirit, in and with us by believing."*

--Galatians 3:2-13

The greatness of our salvation is that our life gets hidden in Christ. It is not our life to live at all. It is Christ living the life through us. We do not have to do anything to earn His approval. We simply let Him do through us. The working of faith is just that. It is Him working through us which makes our faith alive and not dead.

Be honest to God and never lose the touch of His hand

In 1 Kings 13 there is a story of a self-absorbed king named Jeroboam who tried to take the role of priest. He tried to demoralize the people by desecrating their places of worship. He went to a holy place to offer a sacrifice to a false god. Obviously, he was wrong in at least two facets. Firstly, kings do not offer sacrifices. Secondly, the sacrifice is to a false god. The prophet of God shows up and tells him not to continue. The king points at him and commands his army to seize the prophet. Instantly, the Bible says that Jeroboam's hand withered. Like our soul, his hand became useless. I am sure for the army and all involved in that moment that time stood still. Nobody wanted to obey the order to seize the man of God. Jeroboam instantly asks for forgiveness, and God restores the use of his hand.

The same is true for our soul. When we stay honest before God, we will never lose the touch of His hand. He will never leave us nor will He ever forsake us. Will we miss it? Yes! Will we become self-absorbed at times? Yes! Will we sin horribly? Yes! However, if our heart stays honest before Him, then He is committed to restore usefulness to our soul just like He restored usefulness to the hand of this evil king.

I want to close this chapter by drawing your attention to an awesome piece of scripture that totally encapsulates God's heart.

> *"I will not accuse forever, nor will I always be angry, for then the spirit of man would grow faint before me…I was enraged by his sinful greed; I punished him, and hid my face in anger, yet he kept on in his willful ways. **I have seen his ways, but I will heal him;** I will guide him and restore comfort to him."*

--Isaiah 57:16-18

Get the message of this passage! God is saying that our ways infuriate Him. He has seen it all, and He hates man's ways. However, when all is said and done, He has seen our ways, and He chooses to heal us anyway. His restoration is not earned. It is totally by grace.

Friend, God is knocking at the door of our hearts. He is gently reminding us that His heart is to restore our souls to usefulness. We cannot earn or deserve it. It is simply by His grace.

Will you let Him? Will you let Him put you back together piece by piece in order to restore the places in your life that have become withered and lifeless? Will you let Him release the rivers of life out of your innermost being? Will you let Him restore your withered soul into a bumper crop?

✂

Epilogue

THIS BOOK HAS OUTLINED A JOURNEY to the restoration of our soul. Every journey has a beginning. The beginning of this journey is found in forsaking our self-consciousness and entering into Him. It is coming to a place where we realize that we have no hope of righteousness apart from Christ. We have no hope of restoration apart from Him. We need to cross the line and become a fully devoted follower of Christ. If you are reading this and have never crossed that line, then I want to invite you to do so. God is waiting with loving arms to accept you into His family. He wants to forgive you. He wants to restore you. He wants you to be a son or daughter in His family. Christ has already accomplished the life and has done all the work. You simply need to respond to His call. You can do so right now. Just say this prayer with me while believing it from the bottom of your heart:

> *"Lord Jesus Christ, I confess that I am sinful. I have no hope of saving myself. I place my faith and trust in what you did. Your life and Your sacrifice are the basis for my forgiveness. I love you Lord. Please forgive me. Cleanse me from all unrighteousness. Adopt me as Your son/daughter. I asked you to come into my heart. Fuse Yourself to my spirit. Be my life. In Jesus name, Amen."*

Welcome to the family of God.

Ever Wanted to Write A Book?

Inspire Publishing is an innovative new approach to book publishing.

Whilst open to all potential customers, Inspire was founded with the aim to help Pastors and Christian leaders produce the highest quality books.

To this date, publishing a book has been a long and complicated process for authors. Book proposals, low financial returns, rejection letters, and lengthy contracts have all added to this mix of confusion.

However, now there is a clear solution to book publishing. With Inspire there are no rejection letters, and we take no royalties.

So, if you ever wanted to write and publish a book, now is the time. Say good-bye to poor quality self-published books and rejection letters from book publishers, and say hello to the future of book publishing.

inspire
publishing

www.inspirepublishing.org

NOTES

NOTES

NOTES

NOTES

NOTES

NOTES

NOTES

NOTES

Jogi chachen
9387200957